SpringerBriefs in Law

SpringerBriefs present concise summaries of cutting-edge research and practical applications across a wide spectrum of fields. Featuring compact volumes of 50 to 125 pages, the series covers a range of content from professional to academic. Typical topics might include:

- A timely report of state-of-the art analytical techniques
- A bridge between new research results, as published in journal articles, and a contextual literature review
- A snapshot of a hot or emerging topic
- A presentation of core concepts that students must understand in order to make independent contributions

SpringerBriefs in Law showcase emerging theory, empirical research, and practical application in Law from a global author community. SpringerBriefs are characterized by fast, global electronic dissemination, standard publishing contracts, standardized manuscript preparation and formatting guidelines, and expedited production schedules.

Theófilo Miguel Aquino

SOEs and Global Economic Friction

Shifting Legal Concepts Under the Rise of China

Springer

Theófilo Miguel Aquino
Law School
FGV São Paulo School of Law
São Paulo, São Paulo, Brazil

ISSN 2192-855X ISSN 2192-8568 (electronic)
SpringerBriefs in Law
ISBN 978-3-032-00783-4 ISBN 978-3-032-00781-0 (eBook)
https://doi.org/10.1007/978-3-032-00781-0

This Springer imprint is published by the registered company Springer Nature Switzerland AG
The registered company address is: Gewerbestrasse 11, 6330 Cham, Switzerland

To Mariana and Laura, for everything.

Foreword

Choose Your Own Adventure on SOEs!

It is with great pleasure that I introduce this book, which originates from the doctoral thesis of Theófilo Miguel de Aquino, developed within the Law and Development Postgraduate Program at the Getulio Vargas Foundation (FGV).

Although the thesis is, above all, the result of Theófilo's individual effort, it has been deeply nurtured by the regular and intensive activities of our Center on Global Law and Development at FGV. This institutional imprint, in my view, offers a distinctive perspective on the increasingly debated issue of State-Owned Enterprises (SOEs) and their role amid current global geoeconomic tensions.

Theófilo's guiding questions—particularly regarding the meaning and implications of regulating SOEs in trade and investment agreements (TIFAs)—help illuminate how such regulation often reflects a reaction to China's economic model. This approach, however, may have unintended consequences for third countries and their own historical experiences in promoting state participation in the market.

These questions are compelling in their own right. But in this foreword—beyond encouraging you to engage with the rich material that follows—I would like to draw your attention to the multiple ways this book can be read and appreciated. Let me begin with a word of caution: this is certainly not a book that lends itself to summary by artificial intelligence—too much would be lost in the process.

Theófilo's work cannot be captured in a single sentence such as: "*a comprehensive analysis of how China's economic rise has influenced the definition of SOEs in TIFAs.*" While that may be accurate, it is only one path through the book. Having had the privilege of accompanying each step in the development of this work, I can attest that it is a kind of *choose-your-own-adventure* book. And with that in mind, I invite you to embark on the journey.

One possible adventure is to read the book in its entirety, chapter by chapter. This approach allows the reader to engage with the core ideas introduced in Chap. 1, explore the complementary methodologies Theófilo carefully selected to investigate his guiding questions (Chaps. 3 and 4), and follow the outcomes synthesized in the conclusions of each chapter and in Chap. 5.

This comprehensive journey will appeal to anyone working in the field of International Economic Law (IEL), those interested in today's geoeconomic tensions, and readers seeking to understand the impact of China's rise—not only economically, but also in reshaping the ontology and epistemology of IEL. It is the most in-depth and time-intensive route through the book: your longest and most complete journey with Theófilo's work.

Shorter immersions, however, are also rewarding. A first "short adventure" is to explore how a systematic literature review can function within the state-of-the-art of IEL. Addressed in detail in Chap. 3, this alone offers substantial insights into Theófilo's contribution.

The methodology prompts a critical question: how can we map and interrogate the foundations of our understanding in a rapidly changing world? Systematic literature reviews remain rare in legal research—especially in IEL—yet this chapter highlights their potential. Readers can assess both the strengths and limitations of this method, and either pause there or continue to Chap. 5 to see how it supported the subsequent analysis.

Another rich path lies in Chap. 4, which traces the evolution of SOE regulation in the texts of TIFAs. How do legal instruments respond to and reflect shifts in the global order? For those interested in methodology, the case studies of the United States, Japan, and the European Union—each presented in separate sections—share a common approach to systematizing legal language and institutional design.

Unlike Chap. 3, the methodological framework in Chap. 4 is not explicitly stated but can be inferred from the analysis. This type of doctrinal approach is more common in IEL, particularly during the first two decades of the twenty-first century, when TIFAs proliferated. Understanding Theófilo's analytical strategy in this chapter helps illuminate the possibilities and limitations of these agreements in light of a new global economic scenario emerging in the current decade.

Even more concise "adventures" are possible within Chap. 4. Each individual case study—on the U.S., Japan, or the EU—raises specific questions about how major economic powers shape the international regulation of SOEs through legal negotiations. Comparing any two—or all three—of these cases offers another intellectually stimulating exercise. The chapter's conclusion supports this comparative reading, which is, in fact, one of its central aims.

My suggestions for different "reading adventures" might be seen as a flippant gesture, potentially diminishing the weight of the book. On the contrary, I intend to invite you, the reader, to explore the multiple layers and possibilities this work has to offer. You hold in your hands not just a book, but several books in one—each contributing meaningfully to ongoing debates on ontology, epistemology, and methodology in International Economic Law, and more broadly, in law and comparative legal studies.

Transforming a doctoral thesis into a book is, in itself, a testament to the depth and maturity of the research behind it. This publication not only expands upon the original thesis but also offers valuable insights for those seeking to understand the legal and economic challenges of the present.

I am confident that readers will find in this work a rich and indispensable resource—one that bridges theory and practice and speaks to scholars, practitioners, and students alike. Its publication by Springer is a mark of its scholarly quality and impact, and I am proud to have accompanied Theófilo on this academic journey.

I offer my warmest congratulations to Theófilo Miguel de Aquino for this remarkable achievement. Though it is ultimately his own, the book carries the voices of many, especially those of fellow researchers from the Global South. It is also a product of the vibrant intellectual community at FGV's Law and Development Program, to whom we all owe much. Above all, this book is a celebration of the academic universe.

Michelle Ratton Sanchez-Badin is an Associate Professor at the São Paulo Law School of Fundação Getulio Vargas (FGV Direito SP), affiliated with the graduate program in Law and Development. PhD (2004) and Bachelor's degree (1998) from the University of São Paulo Law School (USP). She is a visiting researcher at the Graduate Institute of International Studies (GIIS) in Geneva, Switzerland (2001), and a Global Crystal Eastman Research Fellow at the Hauser Global Law School Program of New York University (2007). She is also a researcher and collaborator at the Brazilian Center for Analysis and Planning (2002–2012), and a visiting professor at the University of California, Irvine (2015), and the University of Sydney (2017). One of the founders of the Society of International Economic Law (SIEL) and RED-DEI (Latin America) and Director of ILA-Brazil.

Disclaimer: Language reviewed with the assistance of ChatGPT (OpenAI); all content and arguments are the author's own.

FGV São Paulo Law School
São Paulo, Brazil
May 11, 2025

Michelle Ratton Sanchez-Badin

Preface

This book grows out of both a personal and academic conviction: that the existing literature on State-Owned Enterprises was deeply fragmented and lacked a coherent systematization. Early in my research, I realized that the debates around SOEs often spoke past one another, and that a more structured, analytical approach was urgently needed. One of my key aims in writing this book is thus to offer future researchers a qualified entrance point into the theme, helping to map out the central questions, concepts, and transformations that define the current landscape.

The work is an evolution of my doctoral thesis, defended and approved in March 2024 at FGV São Paulo Law School. Throughout the years of research and writing, this project expanded beyond the immediate demands of a dissertation into a broader intellectual journey, shaped by critical debates about international economic law, development, and global regulatory change.

In this book, I examine how China's economic emergence has reshaped the legal concept of SOEs within regional and bilateral trade and investment agreements. I analyze how major actors—the United States, the European Union, and Japan—have adapted and reformed their legal definitions of SOEs in response to China's influence, and I trace the broader repercussions for third countries.

I argue that China's rise has provoked a paradigm shift in the global regulatory landscape. The USA, the EU, and Japan, through structural revisions in trade and investment agreements, have moved towards a convergence around the ownership and control framework to define SOEs. This convergence has fueled the spread of a new international regulatory pattern, applied not just to China but also to a wide array of economies from both the Global North and South.

Yet this development is not without serious implications. While China's economic clout drives much of the current momentum for SOE regulation, applying a China-centric framework to the very different realities of developing countries risks creating new inequities and inefficiencies. The book suggests that the expansion of the ownership and control framework may ultimately constrain legitimate development strategies in the Global South, an area that demands much closer attention in future research.

The questions addressed here also resonate with broader contemporary debates about the State's role in domestic economies. Although initially introduced to impose stricter limits on state intervention, the ownership and control framework now coexists with a renewed surge of state-led policies in market-based economies.

Ultimately, I argue that China's influence reaches beyond its own domestic policies: it is actively reshaping the legal frameworks that govern SOEs worldwide. Regulatory clauses originally crafted with China in mind are today impacting countries with vastly different institutional and developmental contexts.

It is my hope that this work contributes to the ongoing conversations about international economic governance and offers a solid foundation for future explorations into the evolving regulation of State-Owned Enterprises.

Disclaimer: The language within the manuscript was reviewed with the assistance of ChatGPT (OpenAI); all content and arguments are the author's own.

São Paulo, Brazil
September 1, 2025

Theófilo Miguel Aquino

Acknowledgments

To my advisor, Professor Michelle Ratton Sanchez-Badin, for her unwavering and steadfast support throughout the development of this work, and for her wisdom in guiding the entire research journey through the inevitable highs and lows of any PhD.

To the FGV São Paulo Law School, for providing me with a transformational opportunity in allowing for the making of the research in the Law and Development PhD Program. The research from which this book originated was made possible by the FGV São Paulo Law School Mario Henrique Simonsen Teaching and Research Scholarship.

To Professors Tamar Groswald, James Nedumpara, Yi Shin Tang, and Raquel Pimenta, for serving on the PhD evaluation committee of the thesis from which this book originated, for all the valuable comments that led to adjustments in the text and opened new paths for future research.

To the peer-reviewers, for helping making the argument of the book stronger and cleaner.

To my lifelong friends, from São Joaquim da Barra to USP and FGV, my deepest thanks for all the friendship and companionship you have given me, and for allowing me to find in São Paulo a warm and welcoming home.

To my family, for giving me the strength to keep moving forward and for being the safe haven I can always return to.

To Mariana, for being my partner in achieving our biggest dreams and for the future that shines ahead of us.

To Laura, the one who has come to make sense of it all.

Competing Interests The author has no competing interests to declare that are relevant to the content of this manuscript.

Contents

List of Abbreviations

BIT	Bilateral Investment Treaty
CPTPP	Comprehensive and Progressive Agreement for Trans-Pacific Partnership
EU	European Union
FTA	Free trade agreement
IMF	International Monetary Fund
MFN	Most-favored nation
NT	National treatment
OECD	Organization for Economic Co-operation and Development
POE	Private-owned enterprise
PTA	Preferential Trade Agreement
RCEP	Regional Comprehensive Economic Partnership
SOE	State-owned enterprise
TPP	Trans-Pacific Partnership
UNCTAD	United Nations Conference on Trade and Development
USMCA	United States-Mexico-Canada Agreement
WTO	World Trade Organization

Chapter 1
Introduction

Abstract The legal definition of state-owned enterprises (SOEs) has become a central issue in the broader geoeconomic rivalry between China and market-oriented economies such as the United States, the European Union, and Japan. China's growing global influence, tied to national security concerns, economic impacts, and regulatory debates, has directly shaped the evolution of SOE regulation. This book examines how these three economies have not merely reacted to China's model but have actively built a new normative framework, the ownership and control framework, to redefine SOEs in trade and investment agreements. Initially diverse in their approaches, the United States, the EU, and Japan have progressively converged toward harmonized rules, which are now being exported through their agreements with both developed and developing countries. This regulatory convergence, while establishing a dominant international standard, raises challenges for the Global South. Countries such as Brazil, although not direct parties in the disputes driving these rules, are nonetheless affected by a framework designed primarily to address China's rise. This book suggests that applying a uniform model risks overlooking the varied realities and development goals of emerging economies, calling for further research on how this framework may constrain legitimate development policies.

State-Owned Enterprises (SOEs) have witnessed a significant surge in prominence over the past two decades. According to the International Monetary Fund (IMF), the number of SOEs among the world's 2000 largest firms doubled during this period, with their assets totaling US$45 trillion in 2020. Notably, 55% of total infrastructure investments in emerging and developing economies are attributed to SOEs.[1]

China's influence in this context stands out remarkably. The IMF estimates that in 2018, Chinese SOEs owned over 15% of the assets of the world's 2000 largest firms, a substantial increase from their 3% share in 2000. In contrast, SOEs from developed countries remained relatively stagnant at around 5% of the total assets of

[1] Gaspar et al. (2020), p. 3.

T. M. Aquino, *SOEs and Global Economic Friction*, SpringerBriefs in Law,
https://doi.org/10.1007/978-3-032-00781-0_1

the world's largest firms during the same period.[2] It is no surprise that these enterprises have been characterized as instigators of "unfair practices" in international trade by G7 Trade Ministers.[3]

In addition to the ongoing debate regarding whether SOEs should be subject to specific regulations in international trade and investment, an independent source of concern lies in the construction of the legal concept of SOEs within regional and bilateral trade and investment agreements. In terms of quantitative analysis, another recent study by the Organization for Economic Co-operation and Development (OECD) underscores the necessity of addressing the ambiguous definition of SOEs.[4]

The study illuminates the absence of a standardized definition for these companies, highlighting the divergent concepts presented by agreements such as the Comprehensive and Progressive Agreement for Trans-Pacific Partnership, the Agreement between the EU and Japan for an Economic Partnership, and the Agreement between the United States, Mexico, and Canada.[5] The study recommends that the OECD address the need for a unified definition of SOEs.[6]

Alongside the study from the OECD, Shima has undertaken extensive research, contending that there appears to be a discernible pattern of selectivity among nations in defining SOEs within international investment agreements.[7] His survey encompassed 1813 such agreements, with a specific emphasis on examining the explicit definitions for government-controlled investors.[8]

His research unequivocally illustrates that certain countries, including the United States (100%), Australia (92%), and Canada (81%), consistently incorporate SOEs into the investor definition.[9] A propensity to include SOEs in investor definitions is also observable in Japan (72%) and the United Arab Emirates (69%), based on Shima's findings.[10]

---

[2] Gaspar et al. (2020), p. 4.

[3] "Our shared concerns include unfair practices, such as all forms of forced technology transfer, intellectual property theft, lowering of labor and environmental standards to gain competitive advantage, market-distorting actions of state-owned enterprises, and harmful industrial subsidies, including those that lead to excess capacity." G7 Trade Ministers Statement, 2022, p. 4. Available at: https://www.bmwk.de/Redaktion/DE/Downloads/G/20220915-g7-trade-ministers-statement-neuhardenberg-15-september-2022.pdf?__blob=publicationFile&v=6. G7 Trade Ministers have in past years expressed repeated concern about "market-distorting industrial subsidies" and "trade-distorting actions by state enterprises." G7 Trade Ministers Statement, 2021. Available at: https://www.gov.uk/government/news/g7-trade-ministers-communique-october-2021.

[4] OECD (2021), pp. 60–66.

[5] OECD (2021), p. 64.

[6] OECD (2021), p. 60.

[7] Shima (2015).

[8] Shima (2015), p. 5.

[9] Shima (2015), p. 8.

[10] It is noteworthy that the majority of international investment agreements, precisely 84%, or 1524 out of the total surveyed, do not explicitly mention government-controlled investors, be it state-owned investment funds or the government itself. This statistic reveals a prevalent absence of recognition of SOEs in investor definitions of such agreements. Yet, in the context of a broader

As I delve deeper into my book, it becomes increasingly evident that the recent spotlight cast by the OECD on the challenges stemming from the lack of a unified set of legal criteria in delineating SOEs is not mere happenstance. It is clear that major economies are actively advocating for a revised framework for defining SOEs within the context of trade and investment agreements.

The discourse on the concept of SOEs reflects the escalating geopolitical rivalries characterizing the international order. Disagreements within the World Trade Organization (WTO) on how SOEs were to be legally defined could explain[11] the erosion of the multilateral legal framework and the emergence of more fragmented bilateral and regional frameworks.[12]

In Ru Ding's study "Interface 2.0 in Rules on State-Owned Enterprises: A Comparative Institutional Framework," the primary divergence of perspectives is outlined, with the USA, the EU, and Japan on one side, and China on the other.[13] In the context of WTO reform efforts, Ding argues that the first group of countries advocated for special and more stringent rules on SOEs, which expand the scope of regulations and make commitments costlier. In contrast, China opposed such proposals, as it is vehemently against any discriminatory treatment of SOEs.[14]

According to Rob Howse,[15] the dissatisfaction of the United States with perceived practical obstacles in determining when an SOE fell under the jurisdiction of the WTO played a pivotal role in the organization coming to a standstill. Howse

---

trend, the number of treaties addressing government-controlled investors is on the rise, particularly in tandem with an emerging inclination towards more detailed treaty provisions. For instance, all treaties surveyed that were enacted in 2013 covered government-controlled investments (Shima, 2015, p. 11).

[11] The uneasiness with WTO rules on SOE is not exclusively about its legal definition. One interpretation, as put forth by Zhou and his coauthors, suggests that the WTO Appellate Body inadvertently contributed to its decline by ruling on the applicability of anti-dumping rules to China, rendering these rules ill-suited for addressing SOE subsidies (Zhou et al., 2019). Another argument points to an institutional gap within the WTO. Wu (2017, p. 682) explains that China can engage in unlawful export subsidies due to the absence of retrospective remedies against export restrictions within the WTO framework. He contends that China's advantage arises not from a lack of compliance or bad-faith conduct, but from the WTO's institutional incapacity. In the absence of retrospective remedies within the dispute resolution mechanism, each WTO member effectively possesses a "free pass for temporary breach" (Wu, 2017, pp. 683–684). This implies that when industrial policy objectives take precedence over concerns about reputational damage, China is inclined to exploit this remedies gap with limited additional costs (Wu, 2017, p. 687). Yet, such parallel arguments are not in contradiction with the diagnosis that the dispute on how SOEs are to be defined played a pivotal role in the downfall of the WTO.

[12] There are still authors who believe the WTO could be repurposed to address regulatory challenges concerning SOEs. For instance, Wolfe believes that the WTO framework has the capacity to demand greater transparency in SOE activities (Wolfe, 2017, p. 728). His view is that the WTO already exercises disciplinary control over SOEs, thus the focus should be on enhancing transparency (Wolfe, 2017, p. 726).

[13] Ding (2020), p. 3.

[14] Ding (2020), p. 20.

[15] Howse (2022), p. 826.

emphasizes that the deprioritization of the WTO legal framework regulation by the USA was primarily due to disagreements on how WTO rules defined SOE.

The rise of regional and bilateral frameworks dedicated to SOEs is not simply a reaction to existing tensions, but a catalyst for innovation in the international legal landscape. These emerging frameworks, as I will later show, redefine longstanding legal frameworks about state ownership in a novel global pattern.

This divergence underscores the intricate dynamics at play in the international landscape of SOE regulation and exemplifies the core subject of my book. The dispute for the legal concept of SOE represents a key case study of an emerging narrative of geoeconomic rivalry between the USA and its more market-based allies, on one side, and China, on the other.[16]

China's substantial influence on these matters has indeed become a key subject of analysis, encompassing national security, economic implications, and regulatory concerns, all primarily viewed through the lens of the Chinese impact on the international order. China's influence affected the development of the legal concept of SOEs, notably impacting major economies such as the United States, the EU, and Japan.

The central objective of this book is thus to offer a comprehensive analysis of how China's growing global influence has reshaped the legal definition of SOEs within regional and bilateral trade and investment agreements. It investigates how major economies—specifically the United States, the European Union, and Japan—have adapted and reformed these agreements in response to China's impact, thereby influencing regulatory practices across the world.

By examining the tensions surrounding the criteria used to define SOEs, the book sheds light on the evolving regulatory strategies of these three actors and explores the implications for third countries. The selection of the United States, the EU, and Japan is not only grounded in existing scholarship that highlights a geoeconomic divide—placing China on one side and these Western and allied economies on the other—but also in their unique normative power to shape global trade governance.

The book contends that these three economies have not merely reacted to China's economic model; rather, they have proactively constructed a new normative framework to govern SOEs at the international level. Under China's influence, they have

[16] The discussion on geoeconomics brings back the realist tradition of international relations to the debate on international economic law. Roberts et al. (2019), pp. 3–5 argue that key to the new geoeconomic order is the transition from a focus on absolute gains to relative gains, mainly because "economic power ultimately undergirds other forms of power, including military power, which are often understood by great powers in relative or zero-sum terms." Blackwill and Harris (2016, p. 20) define geoeconomics as "the use of economic instruments to promote and defend national interests, and to produce beneficial geopolitical results; and the effects of other nations' economic actions on a country's geopolitical goals." There is resonance of more traditional realist arguments based on relative power positions. Mearsheimer (1994, pp. 11–12) has long argued that States are primarily motived by "relative gains concerns," because "states in the international system aim to maximize their relative power positions over other states. The reason is simple: the greater the military advantage one state has over other states, the more secure it is."

redefined the regulatory landscape by introducing structural changes to how SOEs are legally defined in trade and investment agreements.

The key contribution of this work is to show how the United States, the EU, and Japan have progressively converged around a common regulatory approach: the ownership and control framework.[17] Initially marked by diversity in how SOE-related clauses were drafted, their legal texts increasingly mirror each other, signaling a move toward harmonization. This convergence has led to the diffusion of the ownership and control framework as a dominant international standard for defining SOEs—one that is being exported globally through their agreements with both Global North and Global South countries.[18]

This contribution holds particular significance for Brazil and other nations of the Global South, caught in the crosshairs of a regulatory landscape shaped by disputes they are not directly party to. Despite China's economic clout driving the current international push for SOE regulation, I suggest there are relevant clues that the emerging framework could fail to account for the diverse contexts and objectives of developing nations.[19] This raises concerns about the potential inequities and inefficiencies of applying a China-centric framework to the Global South.

While I am not arguing for an immediate impact on the development of Global South economies, the book opens research paths on how the spread of the ownership and control framework could curb legitimate development policies. It presents a strong indication that nuanced approaches to SOEs risk being overshadowed by a one-size-fits-all regulatory apparatus tailored to China's specific challenges. Future researchers should explore the indications laid out in the book to allow for a robust argument.

Such implications come at a time of reevaluation of the State's role in domestic economies. The framework of ownership and control has been introduced as a legal tool designed to make the regulation of SOEs more rigid and restrictive. However, more recent domestic policies by the USA, the EU, and Japan point to increased State intervention in the economy.[20]

---

[17] The role of the private sector in expanding the new pattern should not be understated. For instance, Fleury and Marcoux (2016) argue about the influence of the US private sector on the draft of the TPP.

[18] Complementary explanations for the dissemination of the ownership and control framework may converge with my argument. In Sect. 2.3, I mention, for instance, the OECD Guidelines on Corporate Governance of State-Owned Enterprises, first crafted in 2005, which bring the idea of ownership and control. It is plausible to hypothesize that both the Chinese influence converged with the OECD concertation as reasons for the spread of this new framework. The presence of complementary reasons, however, does not invalidate my conclusions. I thank Professor Yi Shin Tang for this comment specifically.

[19] For example, Brazil's use of SOEs to deploy foreign investment and drive social development operates within distinctly international and national parameters. To see more: Sanchez Badin and Morosini (2015).

[20] There is a caveat needed. The concept of the Global South is inherently multifaceted, representing economies with a diverse array of interests and objectives within the global economic landscape. As my database does not provide a comprehensive overview of trade and investment

The remaining book is structured as follows. Chapter 2 provides an overview of how China is reshaping the international legal order and the challenges associated with SOEs in this field. I identify the development of the competitive neutrality debate as a new regulatory paradigm for substantial obligations upon SOEs, alongside the debate about its legal definition. This book complements the literature about the evolving international legal order due to China's influence.

Chapter 3 is dedicated to the systematic review answering how SOEs are defined within the literature of international economic law. I identify the development of three legal frameworks: the government authority, the ownership and control, and the functional framework. The literature builds the ownership and control framework in place of the government authority as a response to the emergence of China.

It is important to highlight the foundational role of the literature review in shaping the book's broader objectives. This review emerged not only from a theoretical curiosity but also from a practical difficulty encountered during the early stages of my research: a marked fragmentation and lack of coherence within the existing scholarship on SOEs in trade and investment agreements.

To the best of my knowledge, no previous work has attempted to systematize this body of literature in the way this book proposes. By offering a more organized and comprehensive overview, I aim to provide future scholars with a clearer and more accessible point of entry into this complex and evolving field.

Moreover, I contend that the literature provides invaluable evidence as to how the criteria of ownership and control were built to subject Chinese SOEs to international regulation. It shows a structural transformation of the field that goes beyond the sheer intentional positions and negotiations in specific agreements. An opposition to the Chinese economic model is built within the field as a reason for the regulation of SOEs. Therefore, the attempt emerges to substitute an increasingly-seen-as-outdated government authority framework for the market-friendlier ownership and control one.

The literature review shows the main reason why the literature effectively abandons the government authority framework: its practical difficulties in ascertaining whether a Chinese enterprise should be considered a SOE. Such findings are instrumental in understanding later that the best explanation for the convergence towards the ownership and control framework is the deterrence against Chinese SOEs—even if not explicitly stated by regulators and negotiators.

---

agreements entered into by Global South nations, it is plausible that some economies within this category actively embrace the ownership and control framework rather than perceiving it as a constraint.

I express my gratitude to Professor James Nedumpara for his valuable contribution, highlighting India's stance in support of the ownership and control framework. Upon future research encompassing a broader spectrum of Global South economies, an alternative hypothesis may emerge, suggesting that the ownership and control framework represents a market-oriented legal approach rather than being mainly China-centric.

Later, throughout Chap. 4, I offer an analysis of the actual development of rules that define SOEs in regional and bilateral trade and investment agreements signed by the USA, Japan, and the EU, respectively. I demonstrate how the convergence towards the ownership and control framework evolves over time, together with the rise of China, making sense of the structural transformation diagnosed by the literature. I also discuss the findings and their impacts on potential domestic economic development policies to lay out future research paths.

Chapter 5 concludes the book.

References

Blackwill RD, Harris JM (2016) War by other means: Geoeconomics and statecraft, 1st edn. The Belknap Press of Harvard University Press, London

Ding R (2020) Interface 2.0 in rules on state-owned enterprises: a comparative institutional approach. J Int Econ Law 23(3):637–663

Fleury JS, Marcoux JM (2016) The US shaping of state-owned Enterprise disciplines in the trans-Pacific partnership. J Int Econ Law 19(2):445–465

Gaspar V, Medas P, Ralyea J (2020) State-Owned Enterprises in the Time of COVID-19. Available at: https://perma.cc/H2X5-R3EN

Howse R (2022) Official business: international trade law and the resurgence (or resilience) of the state as an economic actor. Univ Pa J Int Law 43(4):821–883

Mearsheimer JJ (1994) The false promise of international institutions. Int Secur 19(3):5–49

OECD (2021) Measuring distortions in international markets: below-market finance. OECD Trade Policy Papers, 247

Roberts A, Choer Moraes H, Ferguson V (2019) Toward a Geoeconomic order in international trade and investment. J Int Econ Law 22(4):655–676

Sanchez Badin MR, Morosini FC (2015) The Brazilian approach to its south-south trade and investment relations: the case of Angola. Denver J Int Law Policy 43(4):489–514

Shima Y (2015) The Policy Landscape for International Investment by Government-controlled Investors: A Fact Finding Survey. OECD Working Papers on International Investment

Wolfe R (2017) Sunshine over Shanghai: can the WTO illuminate the murky world of Chinese SOEs? World Trade Rev 16(4):713–732

Wu M (2017) China's export restrictions and the limits of WTO law. World Trade Rev 16(4):673–691

Zhou W, Gao H, Bai X (2019) Building a market economy through WTO-inspired reform of state-owned enterprises in China. Int Comp Law Q 68(4):977–1022

Chapter 2
The Impact of China in the International Legal Order: The Case of SOEs

Abstract This chapter examines the evolving role of SOEs in international economic law, with particular attention to the implications of China's rise and its model of state capitalism. While SOEs have long been relevant in various historical contexts—such as post-World War II European reconstruction and early GATT discussions—their significance has expanded dramatically in light of China's economic ascendancy. This expansion has fueled a growing association between SOEs and the regulatory challenges posed by China's global influence. The paper argues that China now serves as the paradigmatic case, highlighting the need for intensified scrutiny of SOEs, shaping much of the contemporary legal discourse.

The analysis explores how China interacts with existing regulatory frameworks and the ways in which global actors have responded to perceived imbalances. One such response is the promotion of the "competitive neutrality" paradigm, which seeks to level the playing field by imposing substantive obligations on SOEs. In addition, the legal definitions of SOEs in trade and investment agreements involving the United States, European Union, and Japan are evolving in direct response to China's influence. Ultimately, the study sheds light on how international legal norms are adapting to the complexities introduced by China's state capitalist model.

2.1 Introduction

The historical relevance of SOEs has transcended China's emergence. Discussions about SOEs find pertinence in contexts, such as the post-World War II reconstruction of Europe[1] and the GATT, endeavor to address potential competitive advantages enjoyed by SOEs.[2] Yet the significance of SOEs within the realm of

[1] Howse (2022), pp. 833–835.

[2] Howse (2022), pp. 836–846.

T. M. Aquino, *SOEs and Global Economic Friction*, SpringerBriefs in Law, https://doi.org/10.1007/978-3-032-00781-0_2

international economic law has undergone considerably greater expansion, primarily propelled by the rise of China and its distinct model of state capitalism.[3]

A discernible trend has emerged within the discourse surrounding SOEs, associating China with the regulatory challenges posed by these economies. I posit in Sect. 2.1 that China has come to epitomize the quintessential case illustrating why SOEs warrant heightened scrutiny. In essence, the dialogue on SOEs has been co-opted by apprehensions of China's influence on the international legal order. In Sect. 2.2, I provide a succinct overview of how China seems to be engaged with the regulatory framework governing SOEs.

As a response to the perceived issues associated with SOEs and China, proposals have arisen advocating the adoption of new regulatory paradigms. The notion of "competitive neutrality" has gained traction among regulators, who seek to level the playing field by imposing substantive obligations on SOEs. In Sect. 2.3, I delineate the competitive neutrality framework as a set of substantial obligations related to the multifaceted problems intertwined with SOEs and China.

Furthermore, Chinese influence has been manifested through the responses of major global players, namely, the United States, the European Union, and Japan, beyond the adoption of more substantive obligations embodied by the competitive neutrality paradigm. I contend in the following chapters that the legal criteria defining SOEs in trade and investment agreements concluded by these nations have evolved in tandem with their efforts to deter Chinese influence within the international legal order.

2.2 The Diagnosis of a Chinese Problem with SOEs

Alongside the ongoing transformations in the international legal order driven by China's evolving role, there exists a distinct and contentious dimension within this new landscape, particularly concerning Chinese SOEs. SOEs serve as a focal point for exploring the challenges posed by the Chinese economic model to the established international rules-based order.

This Chinese "problem" attributed to SOEs is characterized by a fusion of geopolitical objectives and economic inefficiencies associated with state-run enterprises. China is singled out as a non-conforming actor within the international order, with its SOEs perceived as instrumental in reinforcing this divergence. This

[3] McNally (2020, p. 2) highlights the contradictory nature of Sino Capitalism, stressing that it combines "top-down state-centric modes of governance and bottom-up networked modes of entrepreneurship." The encounter of Sino-capitalism with the liberal order creates a "chaotic mélange" between "neoliberalism's emphasis on private capital and unfettered market forces with a neo-statist reinsertion of government to manage economies." Coming from a variety of capitalism perspectives, Nölke (2015, p. 11) classifies China as a specific case of "state-permeated economy" whose central coordination mechanism is "close cooperation between public authorities and major domestic enterprises," organized within "competing factions."

perception underscores inferences of political manipulation of SOEs by China and, by extension, portrays countries opposing the Chinese economic model as more neutral actors.

As evidenced throughout the book, allegations of political interference and inefficiencies surrounding SOEs are not unique to the Chinese economy. I have previously highlighted the geopolitical context in which state-backed investment channels by developing countries are viewed as sources of unfair competition by more developed economies. Later, I will delve again into allegations of market-distortion by SOEs. Therefore, I would argue that singling out China primarily stems from the economic significance it has attained, which poses a tangible threat to the market dominance of more market-based economies.

In this context, the economic model protected by rules intended to regulate SOEs predominantly represents the interests of the countries advocating for their implementation, namely, the United States, the European Union, and Japan. Cho and Cheng have highlighted how Western trading partners have exhibited limited tolerance for China's success in the WTO dispute settlement mechanism regarding sensitive issues involving SOEs.[4]

This apprehension seems more rooted in the practical implications of trade rather than the legality of trade. As Trachtman has argued,[5] China's capacity to exert pressure on the domestic industries of many WTO member states in an unprecedented manner has constrained the flexibility of international trade management. This has caused, following the 2008 financial crisis, the Obama administration to initiate a narrative shift in trade relations, while the Trump administration further escalated tensions with China, designating it as a strategic competitor.

Another example comes from the European Union's "White Paper on Levelling the Playing Field as Regards Foreign Subsidies,"[6] which primarily concentrates on addressing the distortive effects of foreign subsidies within the EU internal market. Although not explicitly mentioning China, the paper unmistakably aims to curb any inclination among Member States to adopt the Chinese economic model. This is reinforced by Du,[7] who has highlighted the European Commission's presumption that all SOEs should be treated as a singular economic unit, "the China Inc.,"[8] which emphasizes competition implications.

Chinese SOEs have further become representatives of the Chinese development model. De Kok has underscored the blurred lines between state-owned and private entities in the Chinese economy, casting doubts on the possibility of a trade system devoid of government interference.[9] Wei has noted that China's reliance on SOEs as channels of foreign direct investment and tools for economic development

[4] Cho and Zheng (2022), p. 112.

[5] Trachtman (2017), p. 4.

[6] European Commission (2020).

[7] Du (2016), p. 135.

[8] Following Mark Wu's (2016) denomination.

[9] Kok (2016), p. 28.

warranted special provisions within its WTO Protocol of Accession.[10] There is an inclination to perceive SOEs as instruments directed by political agendas, irrespective of their corporate structure.

Zou's concept of "State Capitalism 4.0" delineates the pervasive influence of the Chinese party-state on the activities and operating environments of Chinese firms abroad.[11] This influence is particularly pronounced in sectors where numerous firms have state ownership or state connections, illustrating how even formally private enterprises can be influenced by the political-economic structure.

Mark Wu's "The China Inc." similarly contends that SOEs are intricately entwined in a web of complex relationships, involving the Party, financial institutions, private enterprises, investment vehicles, and other entities.[12] Wu argues that understanding and regulating the dynamic Chinese economic model necessitates a comprehensive framework, considering multiple aspects of the economic structure.

Wu identifies six significant aspects that underpin his development-model framework. First, he emphasizes the central role of the State-owned Assets Supervision and Administration Commission (SASAC) as the primary shareholder and controller of all SOEs.[13] Second, he highlights the State's control over financial institutions, encompassing both state-owned banks and investment funds acting as holding shareholders of SASAC companies.[14] Third, he underscores the function of the National Development and Reform Commission as the authority for economic planning and coordination.[15]

Fourth, he notes the existence of nested corporate groups, enabling enterprises to exploit complementary relationships and advance state interests.[16] Wu's framework views the structural elements of the Chinese economy as relevant to private enterprises, not just SOEs. Fifth, Wu emphasizes the role of the Communist Party in controlling SOEs and utilizing this control to support various state policy interests.[17] These perceived benefits of SOEs have fueled opposition to the Chinese economic model.

Yingying Wu further highlights two distinct regulatory concerns arising from political interference.[18] First, he emphasizes that conferring regulatory advantages upon SOEs might be motivated by political considerations, such as the State's

[10] Wei (2013), p. 956.

[11] Zou (2019), p. 419.

[12] Wu (2016).

[13] Wu (2016), pp. 271–273.

[14] Wu (2016), p. 273.

[15] Wu (2016), pp. 275–278.

[16] Wu (2016), p. 278.

[17] Wu (2016), pp. 278–279.

[18] Wu (2019), p. 13.

ability to control exports to less friendly nations. Second, he underscores that regulatory advantages often serve political rather than efficiency-related objectives.[19]

These alternate perspectives on SOEs are closely tied to the overarching challenge posed by China to the international economic order. They stress that the perception of countries and authors regarding these challenges significantly influences the discussion of SOEs. The relative positions of countries in their competition with China appear to be a defining factor in their diagnoses.

As Lang points out,[20] concerns about creating a "level playing field" in international trade not only have economic rationale but also play a pivotal role in the political economy of trade policy. The perception of fair competition on a global scale is crucial for sustaining support for liberal trade over the long term.

The perception of unfairness associated with Chinese SOEs constitutes the root for the singling out of China as the main case for SOE-associated problems. In fact, Willemyns contends that the SOEs of developing countries are not a significant threat to an "open trading system."[21] She argues against restricting the ability of developing countries to deploy SOEs as a policy tool based on the comprehensive framework of developed countries, because the actual facts challenge the narrative of Chinese unfairness. However, the narrative of unbalanced global competition appears crystallized in the debate about Chinese SOEs.

In summary, the book delves into this complex and evolving landscape of SOEs, positioning them as a focal point in the context of the global economic order and the challenges posed by China. It highlights the multifaceted nature of these challenges and the intricacies of the global trade and investment narrative. My work underscores how Chinese influence has profoundly transformed the conversation about SOEs and fundamentally shifted the way international trade and investment agreements address this subject matter.

2.3 What Is China's Framework for the International Governance of SOEs?

China appears to be engaged in building an international governance of SOEs designed to facilitate adaptability and strategic maneuverability. Notably, China refrains from participating in the practice of formalizing international jurisdiction

[19] From a corporate governance standpoint, Milhaupt and Pargendler (2017) assert that regulatory issues concerning SOEs are closely tied to conflicts of interest between government shareholders and citizens. They highlight problems of "policy channeling," where the government employs SOEs to pursue non-financial policy goals that benefit citizens but not shareholders. Additionally, they point to the "appropriation of disproportionate financial benefits by the state" (Milhaupt & Pargendler 2017, pp. 478–479).

[20] Lang (2019), p. 681.

[21] Willemyns (2016), p. 22.

over SOEs. It has forged a regional and bilateral strategy of regulation through flexibility.

I found no agreement signed by China that includes a conceptual framework explicitly addressing SOEs, a fact corroborated by Ying,[22] who has likewise identified the absence of such provisions in Chinese FTAs. This deliberate inclination within China's framework to SOEs in the international legal order underscores a pronounced emphasis on flexibility that seems to be spread throughout the Chinese international engagement.

It is important to note that SOEs are not the sole facet of international regulation left unaddressed by China. As suggested by Shaffer and Gao,[23] China tends to abstain from formulating specific rules for novel topics, such as those concerning the digital realm and environmental protection. Simultaneously, they emphasize that China actively advocates for the reduction of trade barriers and extends substantive protections to investors, aligning with its evolving role as a source of FDI.

This pattern of behavior paints an intricate portrait of China's priorities within international legal instruments. Indeed, I have evidence that the literature recognizes this ambiguity as an integral facet of China's framework for constructing international regulation. I draw upon Wang's,[24] Gu's,[25] and Lin's[26] arguments to elucidate this flexibility.

Wang expounds upon his concept of institutional building under the Belt and Road Initiative (BRI), which he terms "quasi-multilateralism."[27] This framework seeks to maximize flexibility through fluid and adaptable legal structures. These structures encompass BRI-specific rules and documents, as well as rules related to BRI that apply to trade and investment, albeit not exclusively so.[28] By integrating these components, China achieves a level of institutional flexibility that permits the selective enforcement of agreements and the ad hoc modification of their forms, contents, and goals.[29]

Wang advances the argument that the BRI's institutional flexibility is underpinned by a three-track institutional mechanism.[30] The first track entails China's endeavors to incorporate BRI principles and initiatives into existing international institutions such as the WTO, the World Intellectual Property Organization, and the United Nations General Assembly.

The second track centers on the development of BRI-related mechanisms, which can be either overarching or sector-specific, and may take the form of multilateral

---

[22] Ying (2020), p. 118.

[23] Shaffer and Gao (2020), p. 28.

[24] Wang (2019).

[25] Gu (2017).

[26] Lin (2017).

[27] Wang (2019), p. 15.

[28] Wang (2019), p. 13.

[29] Wang (2019), p. 17.

[30] Wang (2019), p. 8.

or bilateral arrangements.[31] The third track encompasses domestic institutions designed to enforce BRI principles, exemplified by free-trade and cross-border e-commerce zones.[32]

The Asian Infrastructure Investment Bank (AIIB) stands as an example of a formal BRI-related organization that exemplifies China's framework for multilateralism.[33] The AIIB institutionalizes China's multilateralism through three key principles: a nonresident director system,[34] transparent and open decision-making processes,[35] and a commitment to underdeveloped states by establishing a GDP-based share formula, subscription payment in member-state currency, and bolstered voting power through a Founding Members system primarily composed of underdeveloped Asian states.[36] Notably, significant decisions require consensus, and in instances where only a majority is necessary, members may seek concessions to facilitate cooperative outcomes.[37]

Furthermore, the third institutional track in Wang's argument involves China's domestic institutions established to enforce BRI principles. Notably, this encompasses unique features of SOE governance based on Lin's argument.

Lin presents a compelling case for a networked framework to SOE governance, highlighting the intricate web of connections that these entities establish, both among themselves and with various other types of entities.[38] In addition to the ownership ties within national groups, there is the State-owned Assets Supervision and Administration Commission (SASAC), an entity responsible for overseeing major SOE assets.[39] Beyond shareholder connections, SASAC exerts control through a variety of mechanisms.

First, there is an annual rotation of personnel between SASAC directors and corporate managers to enhance capacity-building and cooperation between SOEs and the government.[40] Second, strategic SOEs delegate substantive management rights to ministries with supervisory authority in the sector they operate in, effectively reducing the gap between the central government and economic activities.[41]

Third, numerous high-ranking government positions are reserved for SOE managers to mitigate conflicts of interest.[42] Significantly, the majority of SOE managers lack a background in the financial sector, as government positions between SOEs

---

31 Wang (2019), p. 10.
32 Wang (2019), p. 11.
33 Gu (2017), p. 138.
34 Gu (2017), p. 151.
35 Gu (2017), pp. 152–154.
36 Gu (2017), p. 154.
37 Gu (2017), p. 147.
38 Lin (2017), p. 584.
39 Lin (2017), p. 588.
40 Lin (2017), p. 590.
41 Lin (2017), p. 590.
42 Lin (2017), pp. 590–591.

are seldom rotated, reinforcing central control and emphasizing the use of vertical ownership ties to coordinate actions between SOEs and national banks.[43]

This domestic environment essentially establishes a state-coordinated institutional framework for the enforcement of BRI goals and principles. Moreover, SOE management underscores a Chinese practice of cultivating personal networks to shape governance institutions.

Graaff's examination of corporate affiliations, policy-planning networks, and personal ties to the Party among a sample of 190 Chinese corporate directors revealed extensive and diverse corporate careers.[44] Notably, 28% of personal connections have transnational reach, with 16% linked to firms in Special Administrative Regions, while slightly over half are domestically rooted.[45] Additionally, nearly half of the sample boasts connections to the Party, and many maintain high-level political affiliations.[46]

These transnational network ties of Chinese corporate directors effectively bridge international business and the Party-State. The emphasis on institutional flexibility underscores the importance of personal connections in resolving disputes and facilitating negotiations. China has adeptly integrated its economic agents into this intricate web of global elite relationships.

The multifaceted portrayal of Chinese SOEs aligns with Du's argument that a rigid form of legal regulation would inadequately encapsulate these enterprises.[47] Depending on the selected evidence, Chinese SOEs can be portrayed as exhibiting both government control and similarities to private enterprises. In essence, the evaluation of relevant characteristics of a given SOE is paramount to reaching a comprehensive understanding.

Du's perspective aptly complements Levy's argument regarding the shortcomings of China's Protocol of Accession to the WTO in addressing regulatory issues related to SOEs. Levy contends that the Protocol primarily aimed to adapt existing WTO agreements to China's specific concerns, even though these agreements were inherently ill-suited to regulating SOEs.[48]

The framework rested on the mistaken assumption that the Chinese case merely extended existing general issues surrounding SOEs, which could be effectively managed through the dispute resolution system.[49] However, this proved erroneous, given the multifaceted structures and mandates of Chinese SOEs.

Consequently, China navigates the complex terrain of international regulation using a diverse array of legal tools, all the while leaving ample room for adaptation and change. I posit that the case of SOEs serves as a representative example of

---

[43] Lin (2017), p. 592.

[44] Graaf (2020), p. 9.

[45] Graaf (2020), p. 11.

[46] Graaf (2020), p. 17.

[47] Du (2014), p. 439.

[48] Levy (2017), p. 636.

[49] Levy (2017), p. 647.

China's path toward a more flexible regulatory framework, despite the more recent inclusion of SOEs provisions in Chinese bilateral treaty protections.[50]

A compelling illustration of this framework is found in the Regional Comprehensive Economic Partnership (RCEP). Article 13.3(5) of the RCEP unequivocally prohibits differentiation in competition rules between enterprises based on their ownership structure. The clause reads as follows:

> Article 13.3: Appropriate Measures against Anti-Competitive Activities (…)
> Each Party shall apply its competition laws and regulations to all entities engaged in commercial activities, regardless of their ownership. Any exclusion or exemption from the application of each Party's competition laws and regulations shall be transparent and based on grounds of public policy or public interest.

This clause exemplifies China's efforts to avoid the imposition of special rules on its SOEs by asserting that they should be subject to the same set of competition rules as POEs. Additionally, Article 13.3(5) introduces the possibility of exceptions in competition laws and regulations based on abstract criteria of public policy and public interest, thus implying a more favorable regulatory environment for SOEs.

Collectively, the aforementioned evidence signifies China's propensity for regulatory adaptability and fluidity. China exhibits a genuine concern for safeguarding its SOEs against overly stringent regulations, while also maintaining the capacity to relax competition rules as needed. Consequently, China does not seem to adhere to the conventional practice of formally establishing jurisdiction over SOEs through explicit definitions in international trade and investment agreements.

On the other side, I argue that key global players, including the United States, the European Union, and Japan, are countering Chinese influence by advocating for renewed legal frameworks. They aim to strengthen the formal authority of international trade and investment agreements concerning SOEs. Issues primarily linked to China within the current regulatory practices on SOEs are slated to be addressed through reforms in both substantive regulations and the conceptual rules governing SOEs. These topics will be explored in the following sections.

2.4 The Effort for Competitive Neutrality

The book focuses on one of the key ways in which the evolving landscape of international economic law is manifesting itself: the redefinition of SOEs in trade agreements by the USA, the EU, and Japan, a development directly tied to China's rising prominence in the international arena. But the field has also undergone other significant structural transformations, primarily in response to the perceived need to address the growing influence of Chinese SOEs within the global order.

A pivotal aspect of this transformation pertains to the substantial changes in the international obligations governing SOEs. A notable endeavor in this regard is the

[50] Sauvant and Nolan (2015), p. 916.

concept of "competitive neutrality," which has gained widespread recognition as an attempt to establish novel substantive rules.

Competitive neutrality frameworks are promoted by formal organizations, utilizing international guidelines of best practices and domestic legislation as tools to establish these principles.[51] Sauvé and Soprana trace the origin of the competitive neutrality framework to the efforts of the OECD to address the corporate governance of SOEs.[52] The OECD's recommendations for regulatory reform aimed to address perceived advantages enjoyed by SOEs, particularly in terms of competition and fairness in markets.[53]

The recommendations, initially introduced in the 2005 OECD Guidelines on Corporate Governance of State-Owned Enterprises ("Guidelines"), were crafted to level the playing field by addressing perceived advantages enjoyed by SOEs due to their ownership, thereby promoting competitive neutrality. The updated edition from 2015 underscores the policy direction for state-owned enterprises, emphasizing their role in maximizing societal value through efficient resource allocation.[54]

This edition advocates for a clear delineation between the state's ownership function and other state functions that may impact SOEs, aligning them more closely with POEs in terms of regulatory oversight and legal compliance.[55] Specifically regarding corporate governance, governments are advised to rely on corporate law that equally applies to privately owned companies. This approach avoids creating special legal forms or granting SOEs privileged status unless absolutely necessary to achieve public policy objectives, ensuring a level playing field between SOEs and POEs.[56]

The OECD proposal on competitive neutrality forwarded by the Guidelines thus seeks to regulate domestic regulatory frameworks as a common ground for all competitive neutrality frameworks. A similar framework is adopted by the World Bank, which advocates for competitive neutrality by evaluating domestic legal provisions that mandate the separation of commercial and non-commercial operations of SOEs, as well as any regulatory provisions that offer SOEs preferential treatment.[57]

In a widely cited OECD paper, Capobianco and Christiansen argue that the European Union and Australia are key proponents of competitive neutrality frameworks.[58] The European model combines regional agreements with domestic legislation and requires the application of competition law to services provided by governments or private entities on the government's behalf. In contrast, Australia's framework focuses on ensuring that no state enterprise gains a net competitive advantage solely due to public ownership.[59]

[51] Ying (2015).

[52] Sauvé and Soprana (2018).

[53] Sauvé and Soprana (2018), p. 616.

[54] OECD (2015), p. 17.

[55] OECD (2015), p. 20.

[56] OECD (2015), p. 34.

[57] World Bank (2018), p. 5.

[58] Capobianco and Christiansen (2011), pp. 14–16.

[59] Capobianco and Christiansen (2011), p. 15.

Competitive neutrality provisions function as a framework that binds states' regulatory tools to substantive provisions designed to ensure—what is perceived as—fair competition between SOEs and POEs. Rather than imposing direct regulatory mandates, competitive neutrality rules provide guidelines for States on how to regulate SOEs.[60]

On the surface, competitive neutrality provisions focus on fostering competition between different types of enterprises rather than conflicting development models. These rules are not inherently opposed to diverse development models but are designed to establish measures that level the playing field between POEs and SOEs.

The World Bank seeks to make policy recommendations that curb what it identifies as market distortions and crowd out potentially distortive effects raised by SOEs. A country's competitive neutrality is evaluated based on domestic legal provisions mandating the separation of commercial and non-commercial operations of SOEs. Besides, the World Bank looks for regulatory provisions that give SOEs preferential treatment, such as in government procurement and tax regimes.[61]

Endeavors to level the playing field between POEs and SOEs are evident in the objective of reducing competitive disparities based solely on ownership. Shima highlights the inclusion of competitive neutrality clauses in IIAs and FTAs negotiated by the United States, Australia, New Zealand, and Singapore in the competition or state enterprise chapters of FTAs concluded since the 2000s.[62] These provisions seek to ensure what is perceived as fair competition between SOEs and POEs.

It is important to emphasize that the competitive neutrality framework is said to not inherently favor POEs.[63] It should be designed to promote equal coexistence between POEs and SOEs, emphasizing that government business activities should not enjoy net competitive advantages over their private sector counterparts merely due to public sector ownership.

The OECD Guidelines and World Bank recommendations do not directly address the central focus of the book, which is the establishment of legal criteria within trade and investment agreements for defining an SOE. However, as I highlighted in the Introduction, it is crucial to note that the release of the Guidelines coincided with the introduction of the ownership and control framework in bilateral trade and investment agreements by the USA and Japan.

---

[60] It is important to distinguish this effort from previous attempts to establish a competition authority within the WTO framework, as outlined by Lloyd (2005). Lloyd (2005, p. 287) argues that a WTO-associated competition authority would primarily focus on regulating the behavior of private entities and SOEs, rather than government measures. Such an authority would necessitate extensive investigations into private actions within international markets, a process that is both resource-intensive and demanding of detailed factual inquiries, particularly when markets span multiple countries. Opposition to establishing such an authority stemmed from concerns about its potential intrusiveness in domestic environments. Competitive neutrality rules diverge from this framework, as they are better understood as a series of obligations designed to bind countries to a level playing field framework.

[61] World Bank (2018), pp. 6–7.

[62] Shima (2015), p. 5.

[63] Willemyns (2016).

This synchronicity implies that the OECD's concerted efforts to enhance competitive neutrality in domestic regulations could play a complementary role in driving the adoption of the ownership and control framework within trade and investment agreements. This effort would work in tandem with China's influence, which I argue serves as a significant factor in this dynamic.[64]

Despite claims of neutrality, there is compelling evidence to suggest that the discourse on competitive fairness may be ideologically biased in favor of POEs. Che argues that the existing international economic order, primarily advocated by Western countries, inherently protects private competitors in the market and discourages government intervention.[65] The significant presence of the state sector in China has posed a particular challenge to this system, resulting in tensions within the international economic order.

Therefore, the economic ascent of China and the push for competitive neutrality can be viewed as catalysts for varied responses, both domestically and internationally. As I contend, the evolution of the new regulatory framework centered on ownership and control is influenced by China's role in shaping the international economic landscape. Future research endeavors should aim to explore its connections with international organizations' advocacy for the competitive neutrality framework.

2.5 Conclusion

Chapter 2 began to indicate how significant geopolitical tensions pervade the debate about SOEs. I have detailed that it is held that the capitalist market is under threat due to SOEs benefiting from perceived unfair advantages by virtue of government ownership.[66]

Special regulatory provisions would be warranted to address these economic imbalances stemming from SOEs. The rationale is that inherent differences between SOEs and POEs demand special rules about SOEs.[67] These advantages would inherently distort market efficiency, allowing undue conduct from SOEs, such as low pricing, monopolistic behavior, and subsidization.[68] The ownership structure of SOEs allows for non-transparent transfers of subsidies and various forms of financial support,[69] including indirect support through tax regimes and land usage rights.[70]

---

[64] I am grateful to Professor Yi Shin Tang for this insightful comment.

[65] Che (2016), p. 181.

[66] Wu (2019).

[67] Willemyns (2016), p. 7. As also posited by Petersmann (2020, p. 12), challenges associated with SOEs do not solely stem from their government ownership per se but primarily emanate from the competitive advantages they accrue by virtue of this ownership structure. The perception of undue economic advantages conferred upon SOEs has reached a point where it is now commonly accepted (Howse 2022, p. 624).

[68] Wu (2019), p. 14.

[69] Levy (2017), p. 640.

[70] Willemyns (2016), p. 6.

Policy instruments may also be deployed to manipulate market outcomes,[71] through less stringent antitrust enforcement and official monopolies on government procurement.[72] Another particular concern revolves around the subsidization of exports. The subsidization of SOEs' products and services could artificially enhance their competitiveness, leading to perceived market displacement and job losses in countries less reliant on SOEs.[73]

However, these arguments should be seen within the larger geopolitical context of market disputes. Crochet and Gustafsson argue precisely that SOEs from the "West" used not to be classified as a matter worthy of specific regulation.[74] They highlight how it was only when developing countries' SOEs became a source of FDI that more developed countries grew aware of the need to broaden the regulation of this kind of entity.[75]

SOEs tend to be characterized as a problem only if they come from emerging economies. For instance, already back in 1992, Fidler had identified US and British concerns regarding the acquisition of their high-technology companies by developing countries' SOEs.[76] In fact, my findings suggest that the practice of laying out legal criteria for the definition of SOE in regional and bilateral trade and investment agreements precedes the emergence of China.

---

[71] Willemyns (2016), p. 5.

[72] Levy (2017), p. 641. I draw attention also to the 2016 OECD's comprehensive analysis of the perceptions of 17 countries on SOEs, named "Concerns Related to the Internationalisation of State-Owned Enterprises: Perspectives from regulators, government owners and the broader business community" (Sultan Balbuena 2016). Thirty one percent of respondents expressed the view that SOEs pose "somewhat more of a threat" than POEs, while 54% considered them to present an equivalent level of threat to POEs (Sultan Balbuena 2016, p. 13). Notable concerns in this context revolved around SOEs' ownership of critical infrastructure, strategic technological and natural resources, as well as the potential for espionage by SOEs (Sultan Balbuena 2016, p. 14). Furthermore, 77% of the respondents express varying degrees of apprehension about "preferential financing," while 61% identify "outright subsidies" as a troubling issue (Sultan Balbuena 2016, p. 17). It is evident that participants in the survey harbor concerns regarding the competitive advantages enjoyed by SOEs vis-à-vis POEs. It is noteworthy that 80% of survey participants express some level of apprehension about "political interference" in enterprises, while over half of them express concerns regarding the "quality of information" and the "risk of corrupt foreign practices" (Sultan Balbuena 2016, p. 21).

[73] Trebilcock and Wong (2018), p. 4.

[74] Crochet and Gustafsson (2021).

[75] Crochet and Gustafsson (2021), p. 3. Zou (2019) indicates as well that the relevance of SOEs to developed countries could be mainly attached to a new kind of development model. Zou refers to China to talk about complex relationships between SOEs and private firms as evidence of a "State Capitalism 4.0" economic model. I would also point to Rajavuori's (2015, pp. 738–739) argument that new kinds of state ownership have been developed as possibilities of regulatory answers against different market distortions. If I put Zou and Rajavuori's arguments together, I have a strong indication that state ownership is a problem as long as it presents a different development path. A summary of the link between SOEs and the development model adopted Chinese case is provided by Pathirana (2020, p. 379).

[76] Fidler (1992), p. 41.

As I expound upon in Chap. 4, I identify that the USA has led the effort of regulating SOEs through formal definition in trade and investment agreements since at least the 1990s. The Chinese impact on the international order has caused a renewal of such legal criteria. It spurred a sophistication of the legal framework, transitioning towards legal criteria of governmental ownership and control.

Competitive neutrality efforts must thus be viewed within the larger context of legal responses to Chinese influence within the international legal order. In the following sections of the book, I will illuminate an alternative perspective in which these responses become apparent: the redesign of conceptual legal criteria to encompass SOEs within the jurisdiction of international trade and investment agreements.

References

Capobianco A, Christiansen H (2011) "Competitive neutrality and state-owned enterprises: challenges and policy options," OECD Corporate Governance Working Papers, 1, pp. 3–31

Che L (2016) Legal implications of the deepened reform of Chinese state-owned enterprises: what can be expected from recent reforms? Tsinghua China Law Rev 8(2):171–190

Cho S, Zheng W (2022) Interfacing twin capitalisms: a communitarian approach. Texas Int Law J 58(2):97–134

Crochet V, Gustafsson M (2021) Lawful remedy or illegal response? Resolving the issue of foreign subsidization under WTO law. World Trade Rev 20(3):343–366

Du M (2014) China's state capitalism and world trade law. Int Comp Law Q 63(2):409–448

Du M (2016) The regulation of Chinese state-owned Enterprises in National Foreign Investment Laws: a comparative analysis. Global J Comp Law 5(1):118–145

European Commission (2020) White Paper on Levelling the Playing Field as Regards Foreign Subsidies. COM(2020) 253 final

Fidler DP (1992) Competition law and international relations. Int Comp Law Q 41(3):563–589

de Graaff N (2020) China Inc. goes global: transnational and national networks of China's globalizing business elite. Rev Int Polit Econ 27(2):208–233

Gu B (2017) Chinese multilateralism in the AIIB. J Int Econ Law 20(1):137–158

Howse R (2022) Official business: international trade law and the resurgence (or resilience) of the state as an economic actor. Univ Pa J Int Law 43(4):821–883

de Kok J (2016) The future of EU trade defence investigations against imports from China. J Int Econ Law 19(2):515–547

Lang A (2019) Heterodox markets and 'market distortions' in the global trading system. J Int Econ Law 22(4):677–719

Levy PI (2017) The treatment of Chinese SOEs in China's WTO protocol of accession. World Trade Rev 16(4):635–653

Lin LW (2017) A network anatomy of Chinese state-owned enterprises. World Trade Rev 16(4):583–600

Lloyd P (2005) When should new areas of rules be added to the WTO? World Trade Rev 4(2):275–293

McNally CA (2020) Chaotic mélange: neo-liberalism and neo-statism in the age of Sino-capitalism. Rev Int Polit Econ 27(2):281–301

Milhaupt C, Pargendler M (2017) Governance challenges of listed state-owned enterprises around the world: National Experiences and a framework for reform. Cornell Int Law J 50(3):473–542

Nölke A (2015) International financial regulation and domestic coalitions in state-permeated capitalism: China and global banking rules. Int Politics 52(6):743–759

OECD. (2015). Guidelines on Corporate Governance of State-Owned Enterprises.

Pathirana D (2020) The paradox of Chinese Investments in Sri Lanka: between investment treaty protection and commercial diplomacy. Asian J Int Law:375–408
Petersmann E-U (2020) Economic Disintegration? Political Economic and Legal Drivers and the Need for 'Greening Embedded Trade Liberalism' Abstract Journal of International Economic Law 23(2):347–370. https://doi.org/10.1093/jiel/jgaa005
Rajavuori M (2015) How should states own? Heinisch v. Germany and the emergence of human rights-sensitive state ownership function. Eur J Int Law 26(3):727–746
Sauvant KP, Nolan MD (2015) China's outward foreign direct investment and international investment law. J Int Econ Law 18(4):893–934
Sauvé P, Soprana M (2018) Disciplining service sector subsidies: where do we stand and where can we (realistically) go? J Int Econ Law 21(3):599–619
Shaffer G, Gao H (2020) A new Chinese economic order? J Int Econ Law:2019–2040
Shima Y (2015) The policy landscape for international investment by government-controlled investors: a fact finding survey. OECD Working Papers on International Investment
Sultan Balbuena S (2016) Concerns Related to the Internationalisation of State-Owned Enterprises: Perspectives from Regulators, Government Owners and the Broader Business Community. OECD Corporate Governance Working Papers, 19
Trachtman JP (2017) U.S.-Chinese Trade: Interface and Lawfare. European University Institute Working Paper, 11
Trebilcock M, Wong S (2018) Trade, technology, and transitions: trampolines or safety nets for displaced workers? J Int Econ Law 21(3):509–545
Wang H (2019) China's approach to the belt and road initiative: scope, character and sustainability. J Int Econ Law 22(1):29–55
Wei D (2013) Antidumping in emerging countries in the post-crisis era: a case study on Brazil and China. J Int Econ Law 16(4):921–958
Willemyns I (2016) Disciplines on state-owned Enterprises in International Economic law: are we moving in the right direction? J Int Econ Law 19(3):657–680
World Bank (2018) State-owned Enterprises: Understanding Their Market Effects and the Need for Competitive Neutrality. https://pubdocs.worldbank.org/en/739371594131714315/15444-WB-SOE-WEB.pdf
Wu M (2016) The 'China, Inc.' challenge to global trade governance. Harv Int Law J 57(2):261–324
Wu Y (2019) Reforming WTO rules on state-owned enterprises: in the context of SOEs receiving various advantages. Springer, Singapore
Ying P (2015) Competitive Neutrality and SOEs Reform: Recent Development and China's Practice. https://www.unescap.org/sites/default/files/CompetitiveNeutralityandSOEsReform RecentDevelopmentandChina'sPractice.pdf
Ying P (2020) Taming SOEs within a redefined competition policy framework: an alternative approach for consensus? China WTO Rev 1:109–146
Zou M (2019) China and the belt and road initiative: transnational labor law under state capitalism 4.0. AJIL Unbound 1323:418–423

Chapter 3
The Structural Shift of the International Framework on SOEs

Abstract This Chapter explores how the rise of China and the resurgence of great-power competition have reshaped legal definitions of State-Owned Enterprises (SOEs) in international trade and investment law. Building on the geopolitical tensions discussed in Chap. 2, the chapter argues that regulatory concerns surrounding Chinese SOEs have prompted a fundamental shift in the global legal approach—from the traditional Government Authority Framework to the more expansive Ownership and Control Framework. This shift reflects not only a legal evolution but also a structural realignment of trade governance aimed at addressing newer, more complex forms of state capitalism.

The chapter analyzes three competing legal frameworks: the Government Authority Framework, rooted in early WTO jurisprudence; the Ownership and Control Framework, which emphasizes state ownership and board control; and the Functional Framework, which focuses on state functions in strategic sectors but has seen limited uptake. The growing preference for the Ownership and Control model—particularly by the U.S., EU, and Japan—signals a coordinated legal response to China's economic model. This chapter thus sets the stage for the empirical analysis in Chap. 4 by tracing how law has become a key arena for geoeconomics contestation in the evolving global trade order.

3.1 Introduction

Chapter 2 revealed how geopolitical tensions have shaped the discourse on state-owned enterprises (SOEs), particularly framing them as a regulatory challenge when originating from emerging economies like China. The perceived market distortions attributed to SOEs—such as unfair subsidies, monopolistic behavior, and export advantages—have spurred demands for specialized trade rules. However, these concerns reflect a selective scrutiny that intensifies when SOEs from the Global South, especially China, expand their global footprint.

Building on this geopolitical backdrop, this Chapter examines the legal evolution of SOE definitions in trade and investment agreements, tracing how China's rise has

T. M. Aquino, *SOEs and Global Economic Friction*, SpringerBriefs in Law,
https://doi.org/10.1007/978-3-032-00781-0_3

fundamentally reshaped regulatory approaches. The chapter introduces three distinct legal frameworks used to define SOEs, each responding to different stages of China's integration into the global economy.

The first, the Government Authority Framework, is rooted in early WTO jurisprudence and ties SOE status to the exercise of public functions.[1] Yet, as China's economic model complicated traditional distinctions, this framework proved inadequate in addressing state influence exercised through indirect means, such as informal state guidance or financial support mechanisms.

A second approach, the Ownership and Control Framework, emerged post-2004, shifting focus toward formal state ownership or de facto control—such as the power to appoint board members—as the defining criteria. Its rise coincides with China's ascent as a trade powerhouse, reflecting a deliberate effort to subject SOEs, particularly Chinese ones, to stricter regulatory disciplines. This framework's appeal lies in its perceived clarity, offering a supposedly bright-line test to identify entities perceived as extensions of the state.

Finally, the Functional Framework takes a more flexible approach, linking SOE status to the performance of state functions in strategic sectors. While theoretically nuanced—allowing for distinctions based on an enterprise's role rather than its ownership structure—this framework has failed to gain traction in practice. Its limited adoption underscores a broader preference for the Ownership and Control Framework's rigidity, which shows affinity with the geopolitical objective of constraining China's state-capitalist model.

I argue that the counterbalance against Chinese influence has driven a paradigm shift—from traditional reliance on the governmental authority framework toward the widespread adoption of the ownership and control model. This shift is not merely technical but reflects a structural recalibration of trade governance to encompass newer forms of state capitalism.

An analysis of the literature on the definition of state-owned enterprises (SOEs) in trade and investment agreements reveals a significant structural shift driven by China's growing influence. This shift is central to understanding the evolution of international agreements, as explored in Chap. 4. The legal transition from a framework based on governmental authority to one centered on ownership and control reflects more than the negotiators' intent—it signals a deeper transformation in the priorities and legal constructs that these agreements seek to regulate.

The field is undergoing a reconfiguration, shaped by the geopolitical imperatives of market power and strategic dominance. China's economic reach has brought these concerns to the forefront of debates surrounding the definition of SOEs. In turn, Chinese SOEs have prompted new legal considerations regarding the structural forms that SOEs can take and how they are incorporated into trade and investment disciplines. This is the structural reorientation diagnosed by the literature reviewed in this chapter.

---

[1]The name of the framework was inspired by Gao and Zhou "authority-based test" from the *US-Anti-Dumping and Countervailing Duties (China)* Case. See: Gao and Zhou (2023), pp. 111–112.

By dissecting these frameworks, the chapter lays the groundwork for the empirical analysis in Chap. 4, where I demonstrate how the ownership and control framework has in fact been codified into a global standard—first by the U.S., then adopted by the EU and Japan—in tandem with China's growing influence. The convergence around this model, as I show, is not just a legal adjustment but a geoeconomic maneuver, reshaping the rules of trade and investment to meet the challenges posed by China's state-driven economy.

In this way, the Chapter bridges the geopolitical tensions explored in Chap. 2 and the treaty-based evidence presented in Chap. 4, revealing how law becomes a battleground for competing economic visions in an era of great-power competition.

3.2 Government Authority Framework

In the realm of defining SOEs within international trade and investment agreements, the first framework that warrants consideration is the government-authority perspective. This framework is characterized by its quest to identify individual enterprises that either exercise governmental authority or enjoy distinctive privileges and monopoly rights.

In essence, the enterprises subjected to scrutiny within this framework must hold a unique form of authority or occupy a privileged position in the market structure, making them amenable to regulation as SOEs. Such authority or privileges may be derived from governmental decree or domestic legislation.

I contend that this framework, while effective in affording protection against competition from SOEs within a particular context and timeframe, began to show signs of obsolescence once China emerged as a formidable competitor. Its limitations became evident in its inability to adequately mitigate the challenges posed by Chinese competition. Two key features underscore the rationale behind this conclusion.

First, the government-authority framework was closely associated with more traditional disciplines such as State Responsibility and the General Agreement on Trade in Services (GATS). As Messenger aptly pointed out,[2] the Articles on State Responsibility, particularly Article 5.37, influenced the interpretation of this framework by the WTO Appellate Body.

However, he notes how it became increasingly apparent that the Articles on State Responsibility provided an inadequate method for determining whether a "parastatal entity" acted on the basis of governmental authority, highlighting the limitations of this framework.[3]

[2] Messenger (2017).

[3] Messenger (2017), p. 66.

The link between the government-authority framework and the rules on state trading enterprises (STE) within GATS is further exemplified by Ying's analysis.[4] These rules define STEs to encompass not only governmental enterprises but also non-governmental enterprises benefiting from "exclusive or special privileges." Yet, the definition lacks a specific and clear criterion for identifying SOEs.

Additionally, the non-discriminatory treatment obligation, stipulated in the STE rules, applies only to "governmental" measures and excludes corporate acts, particularly those of SOEs, further underscoring the challenges associated with this framework.[5]

Second, the government-authority framework possesses an ownership-neutral aspect, wherein both state-owned and private enterprises could fall within its regulatory purview based on their exercise of governmental authority. The key defining criteria revolve around the structural authority an enterprise wields within the market.

As emphasized by Messenger,[6] this leads to complexities in determining when and to what extent an enterprise exercises governmental authority, particularly in evolving social and economic contexts where privately owned entities may exercise governmental functions and state-owned entities might function as private enterprises.

Remarkably, these two features, as mentioned in the cited sources, are inherently intertwined in the data sample, illustrating the complex landscape within which the government-authority framework operates. My findings indicate that the literature, over time, has been moving away from the government-authority framework. The practical difficulties of ascertaining whether an enterprise holds governmental authority have been a persistent challenge, as suggested by both Messenger and Ying.

Drawing from Kennedy's analysis of the *US–Anti-Dumping and Countervailing Duties (China)* case,[7] it becomes evident that the acceptance of the governmental-authority framework by the WTO Appellate Body was viewed as a Chinese success. This interpretation pertains to the definition of a subsidy in Article 1.1(a)(i) of the SCM Agreement, specifically regarding the treatment of state-owned enterprises under that agreement.

China's influence in shaping this interpretation is evident in this literature, and it reflects the ongoing battle to maintain the use of government authority as the criteria for defining jurisdiction over SOEs. Kennedy highlights the *US–Anti-Dumping and Countervailing Duties (China)* as a case in point in which China fought for and won the dispute for interpretation of the meaning of the term public body in the definition of a subsidy in Article 1.1(a)(i) of the SCM Agreement.[8]

In contrast, Blumenthal's work in 1999, for instance, offers a more distanced description of the framework, which was not particularly critical at the time. He

[4] Ying (2020).

[5] Ying (2020), p. 111.

[6] Messenger (2017), p. 68.

[7] Kennedy (2012).

[8] Kennedy (2012), p. 578.

non-critically interprets STE as "governmental and non-governmental enterprises, which have been granted exclusive or special rights or privilege" based on the 1994 Understanding on Article XVII.[9]

Notably, this observation can be attributed to the period when China was still in the process of negotiating its accession to the WTO, and the challenges of applying the government-authority framework were not as apparent as they would later become.

The shift away from the government-authority framework has been largely driven by market-based economies that perceive China as a competitor. These nations are concerned that the framework is ill-equipped to subject Chinese SOEs to adequate regulation, particularly in terms of non-commercial assistance and transparency obligations.

The insufficiencies of this framework were associated with China's geopolitical gains, as it appeared to have found a means to evade regulatory duties on its SOEs due to the challenge of characterizing government authority. This perceived imbalance in competition prompted market-based economies to seek alternative frameworks, particularly the ownership and control perspective, in response to the growing competitive threat posed by China.

3.3 Ownership and Control Framework

The ownership and control framework is characterized by the utilization of three distinct criteria to designate an SOE: first, an enterprise with the government as the majority shareholder; second, an enterprise with board members appointed under government influence; and third, an enterprise whose management decisions are subject to various forms of governmental influence and control.

The core focus of the ownership and control framework lies in assessing the influence that a government can exert over the management of an enterprise, whether through direct ownership or more informal, indirect means of control. This notion of "stateliness" hinges on the presence of such government influence.

As such, this framework is sufficiently flexible to encompass a range of ownership structures, including both direct and indirect government involvement. It also represents a significant departure from the traditional ownership-neutrality stance of the international trade system, as it has evolved as a strategic response to the increasing competition from Chinese SOEs.

Ying, in his analysis of the 2018 CPTPP and the 2018 USMCA, highlights these two agreements as exemplifying the ownership and control framework.[10] These agreements define SOEs based on whether the government holds more than 50% of the share capital or voting rights directly or indirectly, or if it has the power to

[9] Blumenthal (1999), p. 26.

[10] Ying (2020), p. 113.

control the enterprise through any other form of ownership interest. This definition is notably expansive, considering the means of control the government can exert over the enterprise, and extends to indirect or minority ownership.

The TPP, in particular, marked a pivotal moment in the regulatory development of the ownership and control framework. Bhala argues that the negotiations surrounding the TPP's definition of SOEs brought attention to the criteria used to delineate an SOE. The negotiating countries, although in agreement over the percentage of government ownership as the main criteria for subjecting an SOE, could not agree on a figure. The USA was also worried about how the TPP would frame future agreements on the matter.[11]

While countries within the TPP reached a consensus on the key criterion being government ownership, they grappled with setting a specific percentage figure. This debate over the threshold percentage figure primarily stemmed from concerns that certain SOEs from participating countries might be affected. Australia, for instance, was worried about the impact on state-owned hospitals,[12] while Canada opposed the privatization of SOEs central to its cultural heritage.[13]

Ultimately, the TPP included the ownership and control criteria, allowing countries to establish exceptions in their Reservation Schedules. This framework settled on a basic threshold of 50% government ownership, with variations based on the number of government officials serving on an SOE's Board of Directors.[14] This complex framework aimed to capture the diverse structures of government influence on SOEs.

This shift towards the ownership and control framework is closely related to concerns about Chinese SOEs and their unique characteristics. China's evolving economic practices have complicated traditional structural and functional criteria for identifying SOEs.

Shang and Shen highlight the growing importance of public policy considerations in China's overseas investments, which have become a significant motivator for the government.[15] They argue that traditional measures of structural and functional independence are no longer sufficient to ascertain the degree of state control over Chinese SOEs.

China's use of FDI for political purposes, akin to foreign aid, underscores the substantial control that the Chinese government exercises over the investment decisions of SOEs. This control is most pronounced in centrally controlled firms, reinforcing the necessity of the ownership and control framework to address this level of influence. Chinese SOEs, regardless of their classification, remain susceptible to government control, particularly when related to strategic or public policy objectives.

---

[11] Bhala (2017), p. 662.

[12] Bhala (2017), p. 665.

[13] Bhala (2017), p. 668.

[14] Bhala (2017), p. 667.

[15] Shang and Shen (2018), p. 16.

Moreover, scholars like Oh emphasize the blurred boundaries between private enterprises and SOEs in China.[16] She highlights the various tools that the Chinese government employs to exert control over both state-owned and private enterprises, such as party membership for private entrepreneurs and the presence of Communist Party cells in boardrooms. These tools are used to influence strategic management decisions, further necessitating a framework that considers control as a key criterion.

Oh argues that emphasis on equity ownership would fail to fully capture the nature of state capitalism in China, as state influence extends across enterprises regardless of their ownership structure. Both state-owned and private firms operate with limited independence from the state, often aligning their corporate strategies with government priorities that go beyond serving shareholders and employees. The Chinese Communist Party also employs various mechanisms to assert influence over private businesses, such as encouraging party membership among private business owners, providing financial incentives like subsidies, granting informal control rights, and embedding party cells within company leadership.[17]

Stone and coauthors have also found relevant evidence relating to China as to why control and influence need to be taken into account in the definition of SOEs. There would be quantitative evidence to argue that effective influence is exercised by the government upon management decisions of SOEs. They warrant the construction of regulations that impose jurisdiction upon SOEs based on both ownership and control. The political use would be rooted in the amount of State influence upon enterprises.

They contend that one of the clearest indicators of Chinese government influence over outward investment is the issuance of investment guidelines by MOFCOM. These official directives are linked to increased investment activity across various types of firms, though the magnitude of the effect is especially pronounced for state-owned and large enterprises. When a country is added to the government's list of preferred destinations, privately owned firms tend to boost their investments by 74%, while SOEs expand theirs by a factor of 1.9, and centrally managed SOEs increase theirs by 6.6 times. Companies without foreign affiliates raise investment by 68% in response to MOFCOM endorsement, while those with two foreign affiliates increase it by 83%.[18]

Zhou, Gao, and Bai also highlight how separate legal personalities could not be enough to designate whether a Chinese enterprise is acting independently from its government.[19] The idea of control seems necessary, even if it might harm the argument that SOEs have become independent corporations.

In the search for a unified definition of SOEs, McLaughlin suggests that an SOE can be defined as an independent legal entity under control by governmental units

[16] Oh (2021).

[17] Oh (2021), p. 171.

[18] Stone et al. (2022), p. 17.

[19] Zhou et al. (2019), p. 986.

while engaging in commercial activity seeking profit or other strategic goals.[20] This definition captures the unique attributes of SOEs, distinguishing them from other government-controlled entities and addressing the ambiguity surrounding their purpose.

In summary, the ownership and control framework has emerged as a response to the competition posed by Chinese SOEs and a departure from the traditional ownership-neutral stance of the international trade system. This framework combines ownership and control criteria to ensure that government influence on SOEs is effectively addressed. This transformation is evident in various international trade and investment agreements, propelling this framework to predominance in regional and bilateral trade and investment agreements, as I further detail in the following chapters.

3.4 Functional Framework

The functional framework reemerges within the academic literature as a response to the perceived limitations of the ownership and control framework, which is perceived to have failed to address the complexities associated with SOEs. This framework aims to resolve the issues identified in the ownership and control framework, particularly by promoting greater economic interaction and mitigating the pressure against the use of SOEs in various national economies.

I assert that the functional framework endeavors to establish practical criteria that depart from the one-size-fits-all orientation of the ownership and control framework. The key distinguishing feature of the functional framework lies in its classification of SOEs as entities engaged in specific State functions or the provision of public services within designated sectors. It seeks to deter an overinclusive interpretation of SOEs as advanced by the ownership and control criteria.

The functional framework also diverges from the government authority perspective. The authority framework defines SOEs as enterprises that operate under the authority conferred by the government, irrespective of the specific activities or sectors involved. In contrast, the functional framework abstractly defines SOEs as enterprises that perform State functions within strategically important economic sectors.

It is evident from the subsequent chapter that the USA, Japan, and the EU have not adopted the functional criteria in the formulation of their agreements. The empirical evidence suggests that these economies still primarily associate the ownership and control framework with the enhancement of their ability to address the challenges posed by China.

It is worth noting that the functional framework is not a recent development. As far back as 1993, Mushkat argued that defining SOEs based on their purpose offered

---

[20] McLaughlin (2019), p. 11.

a means to avoid disputes concerning the categorization of public and private entities.[21]

He suggested that a functional test could help clarify the ambiguous boundaries between the State and private economy, particularly in the Chinese context. This early perspective on the functional framework foreshadowed the challenges and uncertainties associated with the categorization of SOEs in the context of China.

Mushkat argued, for instance, that tensions around sovereign immunity may arise due to China's often indistinct separation between the State and its state-owned entities, including corporations, enterprises, or state-linked assets like vessels. However, he contends these challenges might have been mitigated through the application of the modern "functional" approach, under which eligibility for State immunity hinges not on the entity's formal legal separation from the State or its institutional position, but rather on the governmental or public character of the specific conduct or transaction at the heart of the legal dispute.[22]

I contend that this characteristic of the functional framework remains relevant today. It continues to be regarded as a more effective means of distinguishing between public and private entities than the other frameworks, particularly the ownership and control model. For instance, Messenger posits that SOEs should be conceptualized based on their functions, opposing the criteria of ownership and authority.[23]

Furthermore, the book highlights that China has been a primary focus of the functional framework's development. China's unique economic landscape and the difficulties it presents with respect to defining the status and legal personality of enterprises have driven the functional framework's formulation. This framework was designed with China in mind.

Both Mushkat and Messenger explicitly reference China in their work, underscoring the need for a more nuanced framework for categorizing enterprises within the Chinese context. Additionally, China's domestic regulations concerning SOEs serve as further evidence supporting the appropriateness of the functional framework for dealing with the specific challenges posed by China.

When discussing various types of SOEs in China, scholars like Zhou, Gao, and Bai emphasize the importance of differentiating SOEs based on their functions.[24] This differentiation is critical because it determines their ownership and the regulatory framework they fall under. The functional framework aligns with this perspective, emphasizing the need for precise categorization and regulation based on the activities and sectors in which SOEs operate.

However, it becomes increasingly clear that the ownership and control framework might be ill-suited to account for these nuances. Under the ownership and control framework, even when the State holds a minority share in an enterprise, it

[21] Mushkat (1993).

[22] Mushkat (1993), p. 42.

[23] Messenger (2017), p. 20.

[24] Zhou et al. (2019), p. 983.

might retain the capacity to influence management. Various types of SOEs are subjected to the same set of stringent rules under the ownership and control framework, despite potential corporate differences.

The functional framework actively opposes the tendency to categorize diverse SOEs under a single umbrella. Its primary argument is that differentiating between Chinese SOEs is essential for facilitating economic transactions between countries with differing economic systems. By classifying SOEs based on their functions and sectors, the functional framework argues against applying the same stringent rules to all SOEs.

Ding's work stands out as a comprehensive critique of the ownership and control framework and agreements derived from it, such as the CPTPP.[25] Her work plays a pivotal role in advocating for a framework that accommodates diverse economic systems and promotes fair economic transactions.

Ding's perspective introduces a type-of-activity framework, which aims to differentiate SOEs based on the activities coordinated by domestic institutions and government authorities.[26] This framework presents two operational options.

The first option suggests applying rules based on specific types of activities equally to both SOEs and non-SOEs, emphasizing neutrality with respect to ownership. The second option posits that more stringent rules could be imposed on SOEs if they are presumed to be coordinated by the government. This normative choice allows for adjustments based on the level of government coordination involved.[27]

Ding's framework diverges from a single set of rules applicable to an entire country, industry, or class of entities. It emphasizes the need to consider the specific type of government coordination in place, offering a more nuanced and context-sensitive framework.[28] Ding's framework would mean a normative choice to decide what kind of government coordination should be subject to regulation. Therefore, Ding continues the effort to provide a substitute for tests such as the governmental authority and the ownership and control frameworks.

The discussion on sovereign immunity provides another illustration of how the functional framework seeks to differentiate SOE regulation. The performance of State functions by SOEs is a key factor determining their eligibility for sovereign immunity, thereby exempting them from legal accountability. This concept has been observed in the case of Chinese SOEs, where their ability to claim sovereign immunity depends on their role in performing State functions.[29]

Chinese SOEs are considered sovereign entities when their ownership is directly or indirectly vested in the state. However, many Chinese SOEs, which do not perform State functions, are no longer regarded as expressions of publicly controlled economic activities. The functional framework plays a crucial role in distinguishing

[25] Ding (2020).

[26] Ding (2020), p. 2.

[27] Ding (2020), pp. 23–24.

[28] Ding (2020), pp. 15–17.

[29] Shang and Shen (2018), p. 5.

when and under what circumstances SOEs should be considered corporate expressions of the State, with legal implications for accountability.

Sauvé and Soprana highlight that an arbitral tribunal considered whether SOEs were performing State functions when determining whether they were entitled to sovereign immunity.[30] This underscores the importance of the functions performed by SOEs in the determination of their legal status. The functional framework aligns with this perspective by differentiating the regulation of SOEs based on their activities and the economic sectors in which they operate.

Indeed, the functional framework allows for nuance that seems unbearable to these nations in a context of geoeconomic competition with China. Proponents of the functional framework may view it as a superior method for identifying SOEs requiring regulation. Yet, this framework may also serve the purpose of granting immunity to SOEs, potentially diminishing the scope of regulatory oversight.

In conclusion, the functional framework represents an attempt to introduce flexibility and nuance into the regulation of SOEs. It focuses on creating a framework that accommodates a diverse range of SOEs that should not be uniformly categorized. By separating and categorizing different types of SOEs, the functional framework seeks to foster a more conducive environment for economic transactions, rather than primarily aiming to curb competition, particularly from China.

It is crucial to note that the book does not identify the actual employment of functional criteria by the USA, the EU, and Japan in their agreements, as discussed in the three subsequent chapters. In my data sample, caveats to the jurisdiction of agreements primarily rely on two criteria, both of which diverge from the principles proposed by the functional framework.

First, agreements employ revenue criteria to exempt an SOE from their jurisdiction. This entails the practice of establishing a minimum revenue threshold that an SOE must meet to fall within the purview of the agreement. The specific threshold varies from case to case. For example, in the 2020 EU-United Kingdom Trade and Cooperation Agreement, Clause 4.2(3) specifies a minimum revenue requirement of 100 million Special Drawing Rights over at least one of the preceding three fiscal years.

Second, a widespread jurisdictional caveat revolves around the ownership of sub-central government entities. Only SOEs under the ownership, control, or authority of the central or federal government are bound by the rules of the agreement. For instance, Appendix 17-D of the CPTPP outlines such caveats for each Member State, particularly concerning "state-owned enterprises owned or controlled by a subcentral level of government."

These exceptions do not align with the principles advocated by the functional framework. Instead, they represent straightforward jurisdictional rules that do not differentiate SOEs based on their specific activities and economic sectors. The absence of functional criteria of agreements thus points to the prevailing adoption of a more rigid ownership and control framework.

---

[30] Sauvé and Soprana (2018), p. 613.

This should be interpreted in light of the broader context of strategic convergence against China. Instead of embracing criteria that facilitate trade and investment, the empirical data suggest that the USA, the EU, and Japan are primarily focused on defining SOEs in ways that enable them to address the specific challenges posed by China.

3.5 Conclusion

I have identified three frameworks in the literature concerning the regulatory criteria to define SOEs. The first framework is the governmental authority framework, which posits that an enterprise should be legally considered as an SOE if it exercises governmental authority, broadly understood, whether through legislation or government directives.

The second framework is the ownership and control perspective, which defines SOEs from a legal standpoint as enterprises with either a majority government shareholding or those subject to effective government influence, such as the power to appoint the majority of board members. Lastly, the third framework is the functional perspective, which holds that an enterprise should be legally categorized as an SOE if it performs state functions in strategic economic sectors.

These frameworks serve as substantial evidence to demonstrate the emergence of a new paradigm for defining SOEs based on ownership and control criteria. It proves that the ownership and control framework has been designed as a means to establish jurisdiction over newer types of SOEs, particularly those inspired by the Chinese model. This framework seeks to subject them to more stringent regulations.

This shift towards ownership and control, as further elaborated in the subsequent chapter, is motivated by a perceived need to deter the Chinese growing influence. The engagement with China has introduced a set of legal criteria aimed at addressing the shortcomings of the traditional government authority framework as China ascended to economic prominence.

The data from various agreements reinforce the narrative of deterrence and provide additional evidence of the influence of China on the development of new regulatory models within the USA, Japan, and the EU based on ownership and control. Although the functional framework attempts to introduce a degree of flexibility by allowing for some exemptions from these stricter regulations, it has not gained significant traction in practice.

References

Bhala R (2017) TPP, American National Security and Chinese SOEs. World Trade Rev 16(4):655–671

Blumental DM (1999) Applying GATT to marketizing economies: the dilemma of WTO accession and reform of China's state-owned enterprises (SOEs). J Int Econ Law 2(1):113–153

Ding R (2020) Interface 2.0 in rules on state-owned enterprises: a comparative institutional approach. J Int Econ Law 23(3):637–663

Gao H, Zhou W (2023) Between market economy and state capitalism: China's state-owned enterprises and the world trading system. Cambridge University Press, Cambridge

Kennedy M (2012) China's role in WTO dispute settlement. World Trade Rev 11(4):555–589

McLaughlin M (2019) Defining a state-owned enterprise in international investment agreements. ICSID Rev 34(3):1–31

Messenger G (2017) The public-private distinction at the world trade organization: fundamental challenges to determining the meaning of 'public body'. Int J Const Law 15(1):60–83

Mushkat R (1993) Jurisdictional issues in a 'highly autonomous region'—the case of Hong Kong. Int Comp Law Q 42:11–47

Oh SY (2021) China's race to the top: regional and global implications of China's industrial policy. World Trade Rev 20(2):165–185

Sauvé P, Soprana M (2018) Disciplining service sector subsidies: where do we stand and where can we (realistically) go? J Int Econ Law 21(3):599–619

Shang S, Shen W (2018) When the state sovereign immunity rule meets sovereign wealth funds in the post financial crisis era: is there still a black hole in international law? Leiden J Int Law 31(4):915–938

Stone RW, Wang Y, Yu S (2022) Chinese power and the state-owned Enterprise. Int Organ 76(1):229–250

Ying P (2020) Taming SOEs within a redefined competition policy framework: an alternative approach for consensus? China WTO Rev 1:109–146

Zhou W, Gao H, Bai X (2019) Building a market economy through WTO-inspired reform of state-owned enterprises in China. Int Comp Law Q 68(4):977–1022

Chapter 4
The Spread of the Ownership and Control Framework in Trade and Investment Agreements

Abstract This Chapter empirically tests the theoretical claims presented in Chap. 3 by analyzing how the ownership and control framework has been implemented across international trade and investment agreements in response to China's economic ascent. While earlier frameworks—such as the governmental authority model—struggled to address indirect state influence, the ownership and control paradigm has emerged as a dominant legal tool to define and regulate SOEs, particularly those shaped by China's state-capitalist model. Through a detailed examination of 194 trade and investment agreements, this chapter identifies a clear temporal and textual convergence beginning post-2004, aligning with China's WTO accession and increasing global presence.

The chapter presents a structured comparative analysis: the United States' pivotal role in promoting the framework; Japan's explicit linking of SOE definitions to Chinese economic behavior; and the European Union's parallel adoption in response to China's emergence as a global investor. It also assesses the global diffusion of this model and potential implications for developing economies. Ultimately, the chapter bridges theory and practice, highlighting how legal design functions as a form of normative power in an era marked by strategic competition and shifting trade governance.

Keywords Ownership and control framework · State-owned enterprises (SOEs) · Trade law harmonization

4.1 Introduction

Building on the theoretical foundations laid out in Chap. 3—where I identified and analyzed the three key frameworks for defining SOEs in international trade and investment agreements—I shift the focus to empirical validation. Having established the emergence of the ownership and control framework as a dominant

T. M. Aquino, *SOEs and Global Economic Friction*, SpringerBriefs in Law,
https://doi.org/10.1007/978-3-032-00781-0_4

regulatory paradigm, this chapter systematically examines how this framework has been operationalized in practice, particularly in response to China's growing economic influence.

The preceding chapter demonstrated that traditional approaches, such as the governmental authority framework, have been increasingly supplanted by the ownership and control model, which targets newer forms of SOEs, especially those influenced by China's state-capitalist system. This shift, I argue, is not merely doctrinal but reflects a structural recalibration by the United States, the European Union, and Japan to counterbalance China's expanding role in global trade governance.

The findings of the granular analysis of 194 trade and investment agreements reveal a clear temporal correlation: the ownership and control framework proliferates post-2004, coinciding with China's rise as a major economic power and its integration into the WTO. Crucially, the data underscores a convergence not only in legal criteria but also in the textual drafting of clauses, culminating in a standardized model epitomized by the CPTPP.

The chapter unfolds through a structured comparative analysis. Section 4.1 anchors the discussion in the U.S. case, illustrating its pivotal role in pioneering the ownership and control framework following China's WTO accession. Section 4.2 turns to Japan, where SOE definitions are explicitly linked to China's economic ascent, while Sect. 4.3 examines the EU's adoption of the framework in parallel with China's transition to a net capital exporter. Finally, Sect. 4.4 evaluates the global diffusion of this regulatory pattern and its implications for developing economies while indicating potential future research paths.

By bridging theory and evidence, this chapter not only substantiates the claims advanced in Chap. 3 but also sets the stage for a deeper interrogation of how normative power is exercised through legal design—a theme that resonates throughout the book.

4.2 The Case of the USA

The impact of China on the pool of agreements of the USA is closely linked to the adaptation of an already well-established practice. The USA has employed some form of the "state enterprise" concept since at least the 1990s, and my analysis of the sample indicates that most instances where state enterprise has been explicitly defined are found in agreements with Latin American countries.

Over time, the USA has modified its legal framework to accommodate China's growing economic influence. I contend that there exists a temporal relation between the rise of China and a shift in how the USA defines SOEs. Specifically, the USA has transitioned from a definition primarily based on government authority to a more sophisticated one grounded in ownership and control-based legal criteria.

It is important to note that this change in pattern does not imply that the USA has restricted its new definition solely to apply to China. On the contrary, this revised framework was notably applied in the 2018 USMCA, signifying the US's intention to employ the legal framework developed in response to China's influence across a diverse range of contexts. Once again, I assert that Latin American countries are more likely to be subject to this new pattern.

4.2.1 The Consolidation of a Practice Before China

In the context of the book, there is strong evidence that China has not prompted the USA to enhance the definition of SOE in its agreements. I contend that China's influence in shaping a regulatory pattern within the USA should not be characterized as an emergence of a new practice, but rather as an adaptation and sophistication of an established one. In fact, the practice of delineating SOEs in international trade and investment agreements was already widespread within the USA, particularly in agreements involving Latin American nations.

The data I have analyzed reveals that the USA has been incorporating provisions to define state enterprises in its agreements since at least the 1995 Honduras-United States of America Bilateral Investment Treaty (BIT). Article 1(f) of this treaty specifies that a "state enterprise" is defined as "a company owned or controlled, directly or indirectly, through ownership interests, by a Party." This represents the earliest example within my sample where a clause establishes jurisdiction by articulating the criteria for identifying a state enterprise.

Latin America emerges as the primary region in which the USA regularly addresses SOEs in international trade and investment agreements. I have documented nine agreements between the USA and Latin American countries that establish a conceptual framework for SOEs. Chart 4.1, displayed below, illustrates the number of agreements containing a definition of SOE signed by the USA per year, categorized by geographical region.

From 1995 to 2008, the USA entered into at least one agreement annually that defined state enterprises. Remarkably, 40% of these agreements (8 out of 20) were forged with Latin American countries. Notably, these Latin American agreements often replicated the language of Article 1(f) from the 1995 Honduras-United States of America BIT.

Even after China acceded to the WTO, Latin America continued to be a focal point in my sample. Between 2001 and 2018, 50% of the U.S. agreements defining SOEs (7 out of 14) were concluded with Latin American nations. Despite the evolving geopolitical tensions with China, East Asia did not emerge as a region with which the USA frequently regulated SOEs. In fact, the USA only has two agreements containing a definition of SOE with East Asian countries: the 2003 Lao-USA Trade Relations Agreement and the 2004 Singapore-USA Free Trade Agreement.

The prevalence of such provisions in agreements with Latin America, a region historically under the USA's geopolitical influence, surpasses that in any other region. In terms of quantitative impact, the influence of China on the US's practice of formal agreements does not appear to be significant. However, this cannot be said for its qualitative influence.

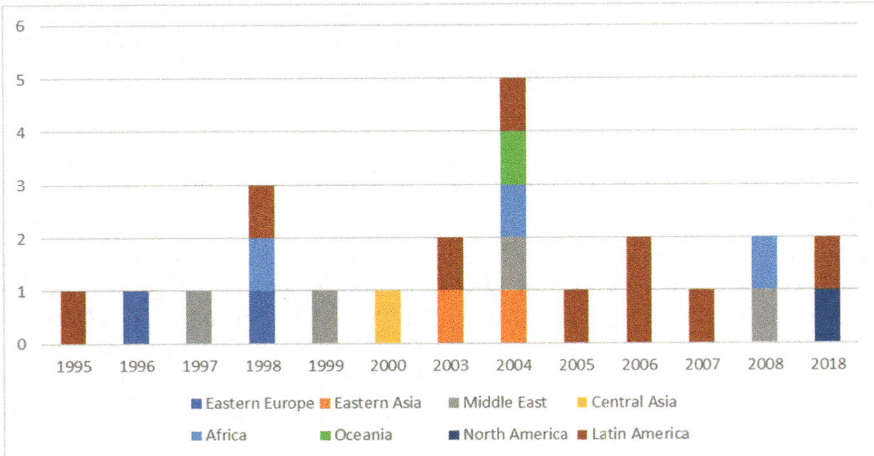

Chart 4.1 Number of US Agreements with a Definition of SOE per Year and per Geographical Region. *Source*: The Author

There is a distinct Chinese influence on how the USA defines SOEs within my sample. The shift from government-authority regulation to an ownership and control-based framework can be traced to Chin's ascendance and has subsequently been reflected in agreements with Latin American countries once more.

4.2.2 *The Spread Beyond China: A Transition of Patterns*

My data sample demonstrates a qualitative shift in the regulatory pattern employed by the USA, one that extends beyond its application in the context of China. The emergence of China is subsequently associated with the US's adoption of the ownership and control criteria, which ultimately becomes the predominant framework in U.S. regulatory practice.

Prior to this shift, the USA traditionally relied on two distinct legal criteria as part of its well-established regulatory practice: the use of the government authority criteria alongside a more stringent interpretation of ownership criteria yet to be mapped out by the literature and thus not explored in detail in Chap. 3. The transition from this more conventional framework to the ownership and control framework marks a noteworthy transformation.

The building of the ownership and control framework in the literature was conceived as a response to the competitive challenges posed by China. The same ownership and control criteria are also observable in the regulatory practices of Japan and the European Union, as I will elucidate in the subsequent two sections. This further underscores a widespread convergence in regulatory responses to the challenges posed by China, a convergence that extends beyond the confines of the Chinese context.

Chart 4.2 Number and Type of Frameworks in US Agreements per Year. *Source*: The Author

Chart 4.2, presented below, provides a visual representation of the evolution of conceptual frameworks within agreements made by the USA over the years:

This chart effectively illustrates the progression of conceptual frameworks in agreements entered into by the United States. The data reveals that from 1995 to 2008, the USA evenly incorporated clauses from both the government authority and the restrictive version of the ownership frameworks in its agreements.

This period demonstrates a notably consistent pattern, extending from the inception of the WTO to the onset of the 2008 international economic crisis. One noteworthy exception occurs with the 2004 Singapore-USA Free Trade Agreement, where a previous version of the ownership and control framework was incorporated. I will delve into it later.

The distinctive feature of the restrictive version of ownership criteria is its reliance on identifying an SOE solely based on ownership interests. This version intentionally omits control as an independent criterion. It presupposes that state control can only exist when there is an ownership interest. An illustrative example of this framework is found in the 2000 USA-Azerbaijan BIT:

> (f) "state enterprise" means a company owned, or controlled through ownership interests, by a Party

The clause above defines a state enterprise as a company that is either owned or controlled through ownership interests. It implies that the concept of state control is intrinsically tied to ownership. There is no indication that a state can exercise control over an enterprise without having ownership interests.

This principle is reiterated in the Presidential Messages to Congress regarding both the 1997 USA-Jordan BIT and the 1998 USA-Mozambique BIT:

> The Treaty defines "state enterprise" as a company owned, or controlled through ownership interests, by a Party. Purely regulatory control over a company does not qualify it as a state enterprise.

Both Messages convey the same content and emphasize that control should not be considered an independent criterion for identifying a state enterprise. Control, according to Presidential intent upon the treaties, is contingent on the existence of ownership interests.

Chart 4.2 serves as evidence that the ownership and control criteria only appear in the 2018 USMCA. This marks the USA's transition from the combined use of government authority and a more restrictive version of ownership criteria to the broader concept of ownership and control—a shift that correlates with China's growing influence.

The ownership and control framework would have also been present in the TPP had the Trump Administration not withdrawn from the agreement. As I have previously pointed out, the literature had regarded the TPP as the model response to competition from Chinese SOEs. Chapter 17 of the original TPP text, later adopted in the 2018 Comprehensive and Progressive Agreement for Trans-Pacific Partnership (CPTPP), aligns with the ownership and control criteria:

> State-owned enterprise means an enterprise that is principally engaged in commercial activities in which a Party:
>
> (a) directly owns more than 50 per cent of the share capital;
>
> (b) controls, through ownership interests, the exercise of more than 50 per cent of the voting rights; or
>
> (c) holds the power to appoint a majority of members of the board of directors or any other equivalent management body.

This constitutes compelling evidence of the transition made by the USA. Control complements the ownership criteria, as expounded in Chap. 3. Clause (d) in the passage above underscores the authority to appoint a majority of board members, even in the absence of ownership interests. This perception aligns with the understanding of the ownership and control framework, where control acts independently to extend the reach of the ownership criteria.

Throughout the debates on the TPP in the House of Representatives, Representative Sander M. Levin laid out explicitly the argument this book furthers. His concern was that a too-narrow a definition of SOE could curb the efforts of regulating enterprises that are "effectively controlled by foreign governments" with less than 50% ownership:

> TPP negotiators are also working on disciplines for state-owned enterprises, or SOEs. Countries that rely heavily on state-controlled and state-funded enterprises are able to give those champions an enormous and unfair advantage over private companies that compete against them in the marketplace. The TPP would include disciplines on SOEs that are expected in language to go beyond anything we have ever included in past agreements, but the extent to which an SOE provision will help to level the playing field will be determined by the degree to which parties seek very broad, country-specific carve-outs for particular SOEs. As concerning, the definition of "SOEs" is too narrow, allowing enterprises that are effectively controlled by foreign governments—but where the government owns less than 50 percent of the shares—to circumvent the obligations.[1]

[1] US Congress (2015) Congressional Record H3554.

It illustrates the U.S. Government's concern with applying the criterion of control—alongside ownership—to foreign SOEs, recognizing that certain legal disciplines allow governments to exercise effective control without holding a majority stake. Representative Sander connects this issue to the unfair advantages these enterprises may enjoy when their governments exploit the previously narrow definition of SOEs. There is a clear intent to broaden this definition to capture an increasingly diverse range of SOE models.

Additionally, it is noteworthy that this transition aligns with China's emergence on the world stage. The structural transformation of the field exposed in Chap. 3 happens right when Representative Sanders expresses his concern with new SOE forms.

The last time the USA exclusively employed the more traditional combination of restrictive ownership and government authority was in the 2008 Rwanda-United States of America BIT, which was signed in the same year the international economic crisis struck. From 2008 to 2018, the USA did not formalize any agreements defining SOEs. It was the period during which the debate on the USA-China dispute was intensifying, and the USA carried out the negotiation process of the initial version of the TPP.

This provides significant evidence of China's influence on U.S. practice. The international economic crisis rendered developed economies more susceptible to international competition..[2] During this time, I infer the USA temporarily suspended the inclusion of SOE definitions in its formal agreements to develop a new SOE framework based on the diagnosis laid out in Chap. 3 that the framing of the SOE definition was structured as a response to China.

It is worth noting that the development of a new regulatory definition of SOEs in response to China had already been tested by the USA in one previous agreement signed with an East Asian nation: the 2004 Singapore-USA Free Trade Agreement. According to Fleury and Marcoux,[3] provisions from the 2004 Singapore Free Trade Agreement were later incorporated into the proposal for defining SOEs in the Trans-Pacific Partnership (TPP).

They argued that the USA utilized the 2004 agreement with Singapore as a foundational model for shaping the definitional clause in the TPP. In fact, the 2004 Agreement with Singapore already introduced the concept of control as an independent criterion, in addition to ownership:

> Article 8.1(3). enterprise means an entity constituted or organized under applicable law, whether or not for profit, and whether privately or governmentally owned or controlled, including a corporation, trust, partnership, sole proprietorship, joint venture, association, or similar organization and a branch of an enterprise

This serves as a significant precursor to the development of the ownership and control framework that later became the predominant pattern. It leads me to the conclusion that as early as 2004, the USA had taken a practice it had previously established

[2] Rolland and Trubek (2019).

[3] Fleury and Marcoux (2016), pp. 7–8.

with Latin America and attempted to sophisticate it in response to the challenges posed by China.

However, it was only in 2008 that the USA decided to halt its practice temporarily to craft a more comprehensive ownership and control clause in a regional agreement—the TPP. Subsequently, the USA took the model it had developed in response to the challenges posed by China and applied it back to its more frequently regulated region, Latin America.

In 2018, the USA signed the USMCA, replacing NAFTA with both Canada and Mexico. Interestingly, the 2018 USMCA employed the framework of ownership and control initially crafted during the TPP negotiations. Indeed, the TPP never materialized with the USA as one of its members. Nonetheless, the model definition of SOEs that emerged from the TPP negotiations found a new application by the USA, especially within its proximity.

In the 2018 USMCA, Article 22.1 provides a precise definition of SOEs:

> state-owned enterprise means an enterprise that is principally engaged in commercial activities, and in which a Party:
>
> (a) directly or indirectly owns more than 50 percent of the share capital;
>
> (b) controls, through direct or indirect ownership interests, the exercise of more than 50 percent of the voting rights;
>
> (c) holds the power to control the enterprise through any other ownership interest, including indirect or minority ownership; or.
>
> (d) holds the power to appoint a majority of members of the board of directors or any other equivalent management body.

This definition notably aligns with the TPP's Chapter 17 definition of SOEs, later introduced in the CPTPP. The USA, along with Canada and Mexico, essentially transplanted the TPP's definition to regulate the treatment of SOEs within the scope of its new regional agreement.

It is worth remembering that the USA traditionally applied a narrower criterion focused solely on ownership. The shift from this narrower ownership-based criterion to the broader framework that encompasses both ownership and control suggests that the element of control became relevant in response to China's evolving role. This change signifies a direct relation with China, which has influenced how the USA regulates SOEs through the application of these rules to different regions worldwide.

Since the enactment of the 2018 USMCA, the USA has not entered into new agreements that would provide additional evidence of the expanded application of the ownership and control criteria.[4] Nonetheless, the mere fact that the 2018 USMCA was established with a direct replication of SOE criteria previously developed within the TPP framework provides substantial evidence for my argument.

The USA, in conjunction with Canada and Mexico, effectively extended a regulatory framework initially designed to address a region more susceptible to Chinese competition and applied it to the context of North American relations. This

[4] In fact, as of 2023, indications suggest that the USA has not been actively pursuing new agreements. See views of then-USTR Ambassador Katherine Tai, available at: https://www.wilsoncenter.org/article/360deg-view-ambassador-katherine-tais-remarks-supply-chain-resilience.

development demonstrates how the regulatory pattern, initially tailored for a Chinese-centered context, has now permeated a wholly distinct regional scenario. In essence, this lends further support to my overarching argument of the emergence of a new pattern of legal definition of SOEs through a framework developed with the active involvement of the USA in response to the challenges posed by China.

4.3 The Case of Japan

I have identified a distinctive pattern of Chinese influence on Japan's decision-making regarding the international governance of SOEs, which partially aligns with the framework observed in the case of the USA. Notably, Japan's response to China's emergence in the international economic order is marked by the adoption of novel and sophisticated regulatory practices.

In contrast to the USA, which adopted a regulatory framework predominant with Latin American nations, Japan embarked on a deliberate regulatory trajectory under the influence of China. This trajectory included the explicit regulation of SOEs in regional and bilateral trade and investment agreements, which had not been identified for Japan previously.

What also sets Japan apart is its early adoption of comprehensive regulatory definitions centered on ownership and control criteria. This proactive stance underscores Japan's endeavor to deter the influence of China in this domain.

Furthermore, Japan extended the regulatory concepts it had developed in response to China to a broad spectrum of countries spanning diverse regions, primarily those bordering the Pacific Ocean. I posit that Japan, by disseminating its regulatory understanding of SOEs, effectively exported its response to Chinese influence from East Asia to Latin America.

These findings provide robust evidence of a convergence between Japan and the USA, and as I demonstrate in Sect. 4.3, the EU. This convergence acts as a catalyst for the development of a new global regulatory framework for SOEs.

4.3.1 The Relation with China's Formal Integration

The explicit relation between Japan's incorporation of the practice of defining SOEs in regional and bilateral trade and investment agreements and China's integration into the international economic order constitutes compelling evidence supporting my assertion that China has significantly influenced Japan's development of a novel pattern for the governance of SOEs.

The inaugural inclusion of an SOE definition in a Japanese international agreement occurred in the 2004 Japan-Mexico Economic Partnership Agreement, specifically in Clause 1(q), which reads: "The term 'state enterprise' means an enterprise owned or controlled through ownership interests by a Party." Subsequently, this practice was consistently extended to agreements involving East Asian and Latin American nations.

Chart 4.3, presented below, illustrates the number of Japanese agreements featuring a definition of SOE over the years, categorized by geographical region of the partner states.

It is noteworthy that China's accession to the WTO in 2001, 3 years before the Japan-Mexico Economic Partnership Agreement in 2004, directly correlates with Japan's decision to incorporate SOEs into its regional and bilateral trade and investment agreements. Before China's WTO membership, I identified no agreements where Japan subjected SOEs to the jurisdiction of its agreements.

Unlike the United States, Japan did not possess a pre-existing practice that could be adapted to respond to China's rise. Japan's initiative to encompass SOEs within its agreements was, therefore, intrinsically linked to China's emergence on the global stage.

Consequently, it is logical to observe that Japan, right from its initial agreements, employed a conceptual framework grounded in ownership and control criteria. Similar to the data concerning the USA, the linkage of ownership and control in defining SOEs reflects Japan's shifting priorities in response to China.

In Chap. 3, I have advanced the argument that the establishment of criteria aligning control with ownership represents a deliberate response to the influence of China. Japan, notably, incorporates both ownership and control criteria into its practices at an early stage, thereby substantiating the claim that this strategic move has been specifically designed to deter China's influence.

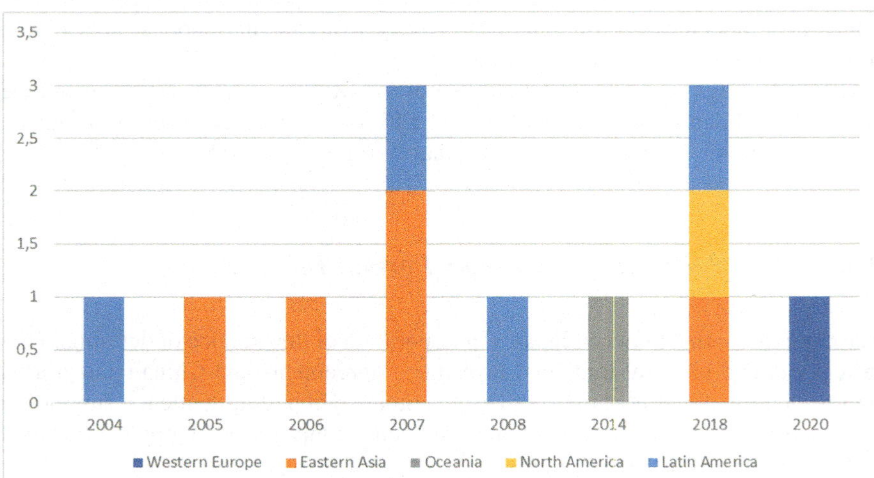

Chart 4.3 Number of Japan's Agreements with a Definition of SOE per Year and per Geographical Region. *Source*: The Author

Given that Japan commenced defining SOEs in its agreements after China's WTO accession, it immediately adopted the ownership and control framework. In contrast, the USA had to transition from prior conceptual frameworks to the ownership and control framework as it adapted to China's ascent.

Chart 4.4 below highlights the relation observed in the Japanese case.

The data clearly indicates that Japan has established a practice of applying ownership and control criteria since its initial agreements involving SOEs. Out of a total of 12 agreements in my sample, approximately 66% (8) adhere to the association of ownership and control in defining SOEs.

The drafting of the definition of SOE based on the ownership and control criteria has displayed relative stability. It appears in agreements between 2005 to 2007 and after 2014. Although no agreements conceptualizing SOEs were enacted between 2007 and 2014, there is still an unbroken adoption of ownership and control criteria.

It was initially employed in Article 95(t) of the 2005 Japan-Malaysia Economic Partnership Agreement:

> (t) the term "state enterprise" means an enterprise owned or controlled by a Country

This clause significantly differs from the clauses in USA agreements, which relied solely on ownership interests and specified control in the narrower context of ownership criteria. In contrast, Japan utilizes a more generic term, asserting jurisdiction over any enterprise owned or controlled by a State, thus encapsulating the ownership and control framework.

Later, Japan has taken the lead in adopting a regulatory strategy that was initially crafted in response to Chinese SOEs and transforming it into a highly effective regulatory framework with broader global applicability. I describe such a pattern in the section below.

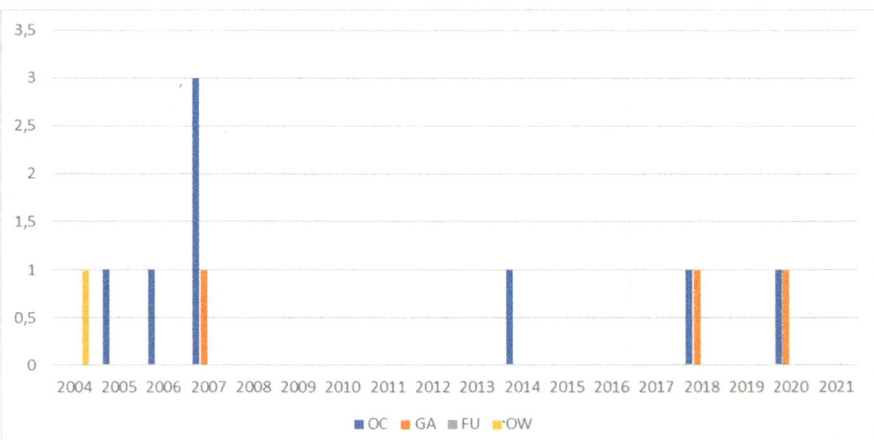

Chart 4.4 Number and Type of Frameworks in Japan's Agreements per Year. *Source*: The Author

4.3.2 The Spread Beyond China: A Strategy Towards the Pacific

The Japanese case underscores the dissemination of ownership and control criteria, primarily across the Pacific region, encompassing nations from East Asia to Latin America. This represents a significant development in the international legal characterization of SOEs, eventually becoming the prevailing model definition in Japanese regional and bilateral trade and investment agreements.

Within this context, Japan has incorporated its SOE definition into one agreement with a country from Oceania, five agreements with East Asian countries, and three agreements with Latin American nations, all of which share borders with the Pacific Ocean. Notably, Japan's four bilateral agreements with East Asian countries that contain a specific definition of SOEs are as follows:

- 2007 Japan-Brunei Economic Partnership Agreement
- 2007 Japan-Indonesia Economic Partnership Agreement
- 2006 Japan-Philippines Economic Partnership Agreement
- 2005 Japan-Malaysia Economic Partnership Agreement

Similarly, Japan has formalized SOE definitions in its bilateral agreements with the following Latin American countries:

- 2008 Japan-Peru Bilateral Investment Treaty
- 2007 Japan-Chile Economic Partnership Agreement
- 2004 Japan-Mexico Economic Partnership Agreement

Remarkably, all seven agreements involve nations with Pacific Ocean borders. Furthermore, Japan has entered into a regional agreement with both East Asian and Latin American countries along the Pacific perimeters, the 2018 CPTPP, and into the 2014 Japan-Australia Economic Partnership Agreement.

Of 9 agreements with Pacific-bordering nations, a significant proportion, marked by approximately 75% (7), incorporate the ownership and control definition of SOEs. Chart 4.4, as depicted earlier, illustrates Japan's consistent utilization of the ownership and control framework in its agreements, tracing back to its initial implementation in 2005 with Malaysia.

My work evidences the consistency in the formulation of clauses within the context of agreements with Pacific-bordering nations that employ the ownership and control definition of SOE. These agreements include the following:

- 2014 Japan-Australia Economic Partnership Agreement
- 2007 Japan-Brunei Economic Partnership Agreement
- 2007 Japan-Indonesia Economic Partnership Agreement
- 2007 Japan-Chile Economic Partnership Agreement
- 2006 Japan-Philippines Economic Partnership Agreement
- 2005 Japan-Malaysia Economic Partnership Agreement

All these agreements feature the same clause within their respective definitional chapters, as read below:

> The term "state enterprise" means an enterprise owned or controlled by the Government of a Party

It is noteworthy that the aforementioned clause bears no resemblance to the more restrictive ownership criteria applied by the United States. If Japan had intended to link control exclusively to ownership, it had the opportunity to do so, as demonstrated by the 2004 Japan-Mexico Economic Partnership Agreement, which explicitly states:

> The term "state enterprise" means an enterprise owned or controlled through ownership interests by a Party

In contrast to the 2004 Agreement with Mexico, which clearly articulated the necessity of ownership interests for the establishment of control, a requirement analogous to more traditional agreements endorsed by the United States, the six agreements above refrain from attaching the criterion of control to that of ownership. Within this subset of agreements, the control criterion stands independently, devoid of a prerequisite for preexisting ownership interests.

These agreements represent an earlier iteration of the ownership and control criteria, subsequently refined and elaborated upon in more recent agreements. This distinction underscores the nuanced evolution of definitions over time. The 2018 CPTPP bears a more sophisticated version of the framework, which converges with more recent employments of the criteria:

> State-owned enterprise means an enterprise that is principally engaged in commercial activities in which a Party:
>
> (a) directly owns more than 50 per cent of the share capital;
>
> (b) controls, through ownership interests, the exercise of more than 50 per cent of the voting rights; or
>
> (c) holds the power to appoint a majority of members of the board of directors or any other equivalent management body.

In its most recent agreement, the 2020 Japan-United Kingdom Comprehensive Economic Partnership Agreement, Article 13.1(h) employs a very similar provision. It defines a "State-owned enterprise" as an entity primarily engaged in commercial activities, in which a Party:

> (h) "State-owned enterprise" means an enterprise that is principally engaged in commercial activities in which a Party:
>
> (i) directly owns more than 50 per cent of the share capital;
>
> (ii) controls, through ownership interests, the exercise of more than 50 per cent of the voting rights;
>
> (iii) holds the power to appoint a majority of members of the board of directors or any other equivalent management body; or.
>
> (iv) has the power to legally direct the actions of the enterprise or otherwise exercises an equivalent degree of control in accordance with its laws and regulations.

The key distinction between the 2020 Bilateral Agreement with the UK and the one established with Malaysia in 2005, for instance, lies in the heightened level of specificity concerning how control is to be exercised. The subclause (h) highlighted above holds particular significance.

It separates control from government shareholding participation. From my understanding, this provision potentially leads to the regulation of privately owned enterprises as if they were state-owned, provided for instance that industrial policies grant the government the authority to influence and guide their actions of private enterprises. The Agreement refrains from specifying the degree of direction necessary to trigger the application of Article 13.1(h)(iv). However, it expressly leaves open the legal possibility for such regulation.

This refined articulation closely mirrors the conceptual framework introduced in the 2018 USMCA. The consistent trajectory underscores the robust evidence of the widespread adoption of a regulatory framework originally designed to deter China's influence.

What is particularly striking is that the ownership and control definition is not exclusive to Japan but has also been embraced by the United States, as well as the European Union. A framework designed in response to China, as argued in Chap. 3, has effectively been turned into a new regulatory pattern.

4.4 The Case of the EU

A similar trend in argumentation is discernible when examining the regulatory frameworks adopted by the EU. The definitions of SOEs found within EU agreements exhibit a pronounced alignment with the rise of China in the global economy, serving as a strategic response to counterbalance China's influence. Simultaneously, it becomes apparent that the measures devised to address China's ascent have been disseminated widely.

The dataset pertaining to the EU offers compelling evidence supporting my assertions. First, within the scope of my database analysis, the EU emerges as a distinctive international actor that has, in principle, endorsed an investment agreement with China. In stark contrast, both the USA and Japan lack any signed agreement with China, not even in principle.

This empirical observation emboldens the contention that the regulatory framework in question has been purposefully crafted with China in mind, subsequently permeating the international arena as a prevailing normative pattern. It furnishes conclusive evidence that when engaging in investment agreements with China, the ownership and control framework is consistently chosen as the framework for delineating SOEs.

Second, it is worth highlighting the congruence between the EU, the USA, and Japan in their fundamental framework on this issue. The criteria of ownership and control have been integrated into the EU's agreements, coinciding with China's consolidation as a significant source of FDI. This alignment reflects a convergence in regulatory patterns, akin to those embraced by Japan and the USA. China, therefore, emerges as a central explanatory factor behind the development of a novel regulatory model, one that the EU has also adopted.

Third, this alignment of regulatory frameworks across different regions underscores the pervasive impact of China's economic emergence on the evolution of international trade agreements and norms. It reflects a shared strategic response to the challenges and opportunities posed by China's ascendance in the global economy, a response that has drawn in countries facing diverse challenges that do not mirror those posed by China.

4.4.1 The Relation with the Rise of Chinese FDI

The data pertaining to the EU reveals a discernible pattern in its framework for defining SOEs within regional and bilateral trade and investment agreements. The EU has progressively converged towards a regulatory practice resembling that of the United States and Japan, characterized by the articulation of clear legal criteria for identifying SOEs. This convergence underscores China's role in the dissemination of this novel regulatory practice.

In my dataset, there is no instance of the EU defining SOEs before 2011, a crucial year when China transitioned from being a capital importer to becoming a substantial capital exporter. Data from the World Bank clearly indicates a substantial surge in China's FDI outflows commencing in 2011, as evident from its balance of payments (Chart 4.5).

The year 2011 marks a pivotal turning point for China's net FDI outflows, as its levels stabilized above 50 billion dollars and began an upward trajectory, reaching a

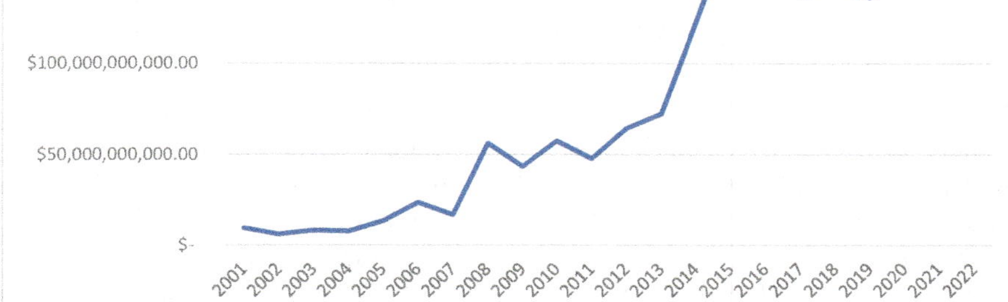

Chart 4.5 Foreign Direct Investment, Net Outflows (Balance of Payments, current US$)—China. *Source*: The World Bank Data (2023). Available at: https://data.worldbank.org/indicator/BM.KLT.DINV.CD.WD?contextual=default&end=2022&locations=CN&start=2001&view=chart

zenith in 2016, surpassing 200 billion dollars. This upward trajectory in Chinese FDI outflows correlates significantly with the EU's practice of defining SOEs in its agreements.

A direct relation emerges between the EU's first agreement defining SOEs and the year when China established itself as a net international investment source. Notably, the 2011 EU-Korea Free Trade Agreement stands as the inaugural instance of such a definition within the sample.

In this agreement, SOEs are mentioned to create a caveat within the jurisdiction regarding electronic products, identifying a "State-Owned National Electronic/Information System." This is primarily defined based on the exercise of regulatory functions and powers of the government, thus aligning with a government-authority framework, although it remains somewhat superficial in its treatment:

> State-Owned National Electronic/Information System
>
> Unbound for measures affecting the administration and operation of any state-owned electronic information system that contains proprietary government information or information gathered pursuant to the regulatory functions and powers of the government. This reservation does not apply to payment and settlement systems related to financial services.

It is only in the 2014 EU-Ukraine Association Agreement that the EU furnishes a more comprehensive definition of SOEs. In this instance, SOEs are defined with a focus on their participation in the privatization of Ukrainian enterprises, contingent upon state ownership exceeding 25%, as laid out in Appendix XVI-D to Chap. 6:

> The acquisition of state-owned properties
>
> Enterprises and governmental agencies in which state ownership exceeds 25% are not authorized to participate in the privatization of Ukrainian enterprises.

Subsequently, in the 2020 EU-United Kingdom Trade and Cooperation Agreement, the EU takes a more sophisticated framework to defining SOEs, incorporating a fully developed ownership and control-based framework.

> Article 4.1(1)(j) "State-owned enterprise" means an enterprise in which a Party:
>
> (i) directly owns more than 50% of the share capital;
>
> (ii) controls, directly or indirectly, the exercise of more than 50% of the voting rights;
>
> (iii) holds the power to appoint a majority of the members of the board of directors or any other equivalent management body; or.
>
> (iv) has the power to exercise control over the enterprise. For the establishment of control, all relevant legal and factual elements shall be taken into account on a case-by-case basis.

The relation between the rise of Chinese FDI outflows and the EU's adoption of a practice involving the establishment of legal criteria for defining SOEs within its agreements is striking. Clauses defining SOEs only appear in the EU's practice after China had already established itself as a net exporter of capital.

Despite the EU being a latecomer compared to the United States and Japan in adopting the ownership and control framework, the temporal discrepancy does not diminish its significance as particularly compelling evidence supporting the argument that this regulatory framework has been strategically formulated in response to China and subsequently employed comprehensively.

A pivotal development in this regard is the 2020 EU-China Comprehensive Agreement in Principle on Investment, explicitly articulating the intent to define SOEs through both the government authority framework and the ownership and control paradigm. While the government authority framework has been a prevailing framework predating China's accession to the WTO, its persistence in the contemporary practices of the USA, Japan, and the EU does not seem to offer additional analytical value.

The crux of significance within the EU dataset lies in the discernible application of the ownership and control criteria specifically directed towards China. In Section 3 of the Agreement, titled "Level Playing Field related Commitments," explicit provisions are outlined for SOEs:

> State-owned Enterprises (…).
>
> These disciplines cover a broadly defined category of 'state-owned enterprises', which includes entities controlled by the state through minority ownership or legal title, as well as state designated monopolies or entities vested with special rights or privileges. The rules aim to improve the level playing field between public and private companies. This should contribute to fairer competition on the market and have a favourable effect on investor confidence.

These regulations encompass a broad category of such entities, including those controlled by the state through minority ownership or legal title, state-designated monopolies, or entities vested with special rights or privileges. The Agreement in Principle formalizes the EU's intention to subject SOEs to the jurisdiction of the final text, even if not directly owned by the State but controlled through minority ownership or legal title. The expansion of control criteria alongside ownership criteria underscores the EU's strategic utilization of the ownership and control framework as a remedy against China.

Furthermore, the EU dataset extends its regulatory endeavors across diverse contexts, prominently featuring agreements with Eastern European and Eastern Asian countries, as detailed in the subsequent section. This multifaceted engagement lends support to the assertion that the EU's overarching regulatory practice is primarily oriented towards China, thus establishing itself as a broader regulatory paradigm shaped under the influence of China.

In the subsequent section, I expound upon this argument by delving deeper into the impact and implications of this regulatory practice influenced by China, highlighting the convergence towards a pattern of ownership and control criteria. The EU follows the path of the USA and Japan in applying the ownership and control framework as the model regulation of SOEs.

4.4.2 *The Spread Beyond China: A Robust Pattern of Diffusion*

Beyond its application within the 2020 Agreement in Principle with China, the EU has consciously paralleled the United States and Japan, cementing the ownership and control framework as the predominant regulatory framework in both its bilateral and regional trade and investment agreements. The data evidence that the EU has acted as a consistent architect of a new global framework on SOEs based on the ownership and control criteria.

The EU has actively disseminated this framework from East Asia to both East and West Europe, extending its influence to North America. Particularly, five out of seven agreements utilizing the ownership and control framework were signed with nations from Eastern Europe or East Asia, namely, China, Japan, Armenia, Kazakhstan, and Ukraine. The remaining two agreements involve Canada and the United Kingdom.

This diffusion pattern surpasses that of both the United States and Japan, as illustrated in Chart 4.6, highlighting the geographical diversity of agreements signed throughout the years.

Among the eight agreements signed between 2011 and 2021, wherein the EU explicitly defined SOEs, an overwhelming 75% (6 agreements) applied the ownership and control criteria. The seven agreements are:

- 2020 EU-China Comprehensive Agreement on Investment[5]
- 2020 EU-United Kingdom Trade and Cooperation Agreement
- 2018 EU-Japan Economic Partnership Agreement
- 2017 EU-Armenia Comprehensive and Enhanced Partnership Agreement
- 2017 Comprehensive Trade and Economic Agreements between Canada and the European Union (CETA)[6]
- 2015 EU-Kazakhstan Enhanced Partnership and Cooperation Agreement
- 2014 EU-Ukraine Association Agreement

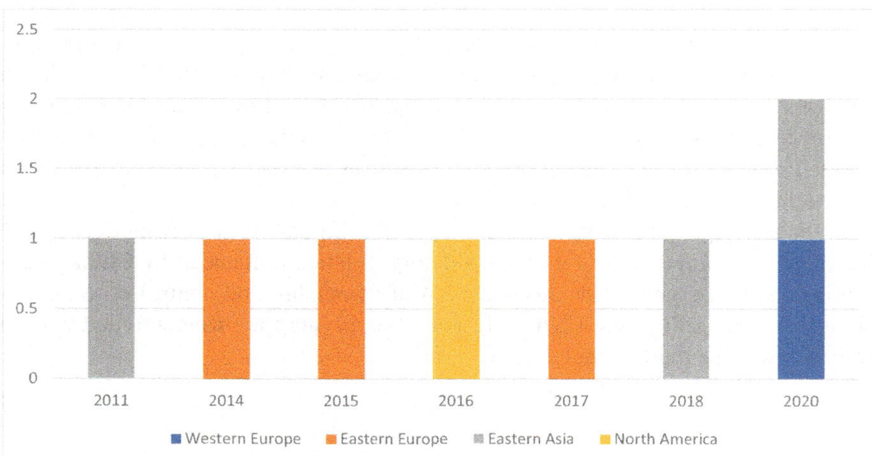

Chart 4.6 Number of EU Agreements with a Definition of SOE per Year and per Geographical Region. *Source*: The Author

[5] Agreement in principle.

[6] Entry into force progressively from 2017 onwards.

Chart 4.7 below displays the employment of regulatory frameworks in the timelapse since then. It calls attention to the predominance of the ownership and control framework.

The notable exception is the 2010 EU-Korea Free Trade Agreement, as outlined in the previous section, which applied solely to the government authority framework. However, since the 2014 EU-Ukraine Association Agreement, all subsequent agreements in which the EU defined SOEs uniformly employed the ownership and control framework.

Even in its incipient stages, such as in the 2017 CETA, the notion of ownership and control was evident. Article 1.1 reads as follows:

> Article 1.1 State-enterprise means an enterprise that is either owned or controlled by a Party.

A tentative version of a more comprehensive ownership and control framework appears for the first time in the 2015 EU-Kazakhstan Enhanced Partnership and Cooperation Agreement. Within Article 163, one reads a previous version of the same criteria, which were later applied by the EU and in agreements with the USA and Japan:

> Article 163(…).
>
> (a) 'state-owned enterprise' means any enterprise involved in a commercial activity over which a Party at central or subcentral level owns more than 50 of the enterprise's subscribed capital or the votes attached to the shares issued by the enterprise;
>
> (b) 'state-controlled enterprise' means any enterprise involved in a commercial activity over which a Party at central or sub-central level exercises or has the possibility of exercising decisive influence, directly or indirectly, by virtue of its financial participation therein or by the rules or practices on its functioning, or by any other means relevant to establish such decisive influence. Decisive influence on the part of a Party shall be presumed when a Party, directly or indirectly, can appoint more than half of the members of the enterprise's administrative, managerial or supervisory body.

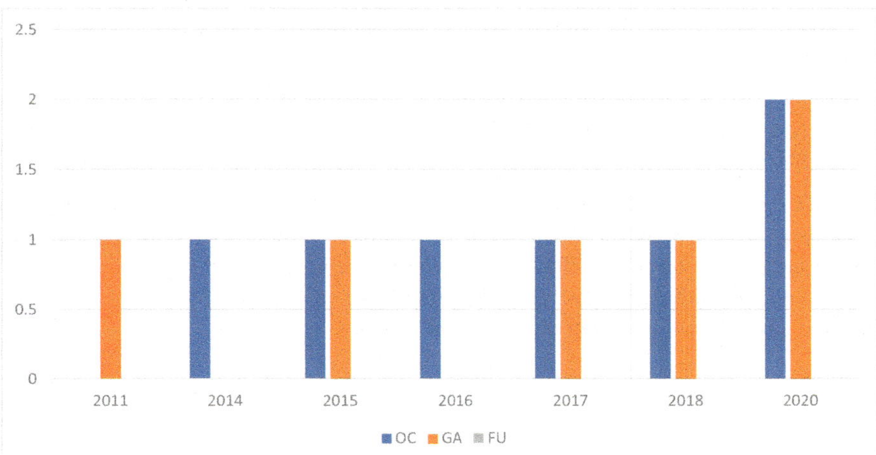

Chart 4.7 Number and Type of Frameworks in the EU's Agreements per Year. *Source*: The Author

The legal framework is visible, although structured in a slightly different way. The 2015 Agreement with Kazakhstan differentiates between state-owned and state-controlled enterprises, whereas a more consolidated version of the framework collapses both ownership and control in the definition of SOE.

The legal framework, as seen in the 2015 EU-Kazakhstan Enhanced Partnership and Cooperation Agreement, laid the groundwork for a more consolidated version that emerged in the 2017 EU-Armenia Comprehensive and Enhanced Partnership Agreement. Its Article 301(a) follows the same pattern as the 2018 USCMA and the 2020 Japan-United Kingdom Comprehensive Economic Partnership Agreement:

> (a) "state-owned enterprise" means an enterprise, including any subsidiary, in which a Party, directly or indirectly:
>
> (i) owns more than 50% of the enterprise's subscribed capital or controls more than 50% of the votes attached to the shares issued by the enterprise;
>
> (ii) can appoint more than half of the members of the enterprise's board of directors or an equivalent body; or.
>
> (iii) can exercise control over the enterprise.

The convergence of clauses with the 2018 USCMA and the 2020 Japan-United Kingdom Comprehensive Economic Partnership Agreement further underlines a consistent trend in describing SOEs based on ownership and control criteria. This alignment underscores the EU's strategic adoption of the ownership and control framework, not only in response to Chinese SOEs but also as a predominant regulatory tool to expand its influence geographically.

In fact, the 2018 EU-Japan Economic Partnership Agreement consolidates the convergence between the EU and Japan with another identical ownership and control framework:

> Article 13.1(...).
>
> (h) "state-owned enterprise" means an enterprise that is engaged in commercial activities in which a Party:
>
> (i) directly owns more than 50 per cent of the share capital;
>
> (ii) controls, directly or indirectly through ownership interests, the exercise of more than 50 per cent of the voting rights;
>
> iii) holds the power to appoint a majority of members of the board of directors or any other equivalent management body; or
>
> (iv) has the power to legally direct the actions of the enterprise or otherwise exercises an equivalent degree of control in accordance with its laws and regulations.

The EU's strategic adoption of the ownership and control framework, not only as a response to Chinese SOEs but also as a predominant regulatory paradigm, signals a deliberate expansion of its influence across diverse geopolitical regions. This trend is not only robust but also distinguishes the EU's regulatory approach as a comprehensive and influential model on the global stage.

4.5 Conclusion

A comprehensive analysis of regional and bilateral trade and investment agreements signed by the USA, the EU, and Japan reveals a consistent adoption of the ownership and control framework. These major players have strategically applied ownership and control criteria in various agreements, establishing it as the prevailing regulatory pattern.

Importantly, there is a direct relation between the implementation of this framework and pivotal junctures in China's economic progression. Furthermore, I contend that the restructuring of the definition of SOEs within trade and investment agreements presents indications of potential ramifications for domestic politics and economies across both the Global North and South, which could be further explored by future researchers.

The USA presented a case of transition of patterns. It had employed the more traditional government-authority framework in agreements primarily directed towards Latin America. My data shows that it halts the signing of agreements in 2008—the year of the economic crash. The USA resumes the celebration of agreements in 2018 with the 2018 USCMA.

Such a halt is explainable by a perceived need to respond to regulatory challenges brought by China. In a testimony before the U.S. Senate Committee on Banking, Housing, and Urban Affairs, Dennis Shea, then Chairman of the United States-China Economic Security Review Commission, underscored that China's accession to the WTO had failed to enhance U.S. national security through market liberalization.[7] Blustein reports that by 2009, briefing sessions with former President Barack Obama explored complaints from the business community regarding "Chinese practices."[8]

Raj Bhala highlights how the American political elite rallied to support the necessity of regulatory measures against national security threats posed by Chinese SOEs.[9] At the time, the TPP was seen as the solution. Initially, a group of four Secretaries of State emphasized that the TPP was a mere deal affecting trade barriers and tariff rates, as it would also effectively enhance the US national security.[10]

Subsequently, eight former Secretaries of Defense joined to argue that the TPP assists in the containment of China.[11] This demonstrates that Chinese SOEs indeed raise national security concerns, even though the exact definition of national security remains somewhat elusive. The TPP serves as an illustrative case of regulatory developments that were, at least in part, justified by such concerns.

The USA halted its agreements to build a new legal definition of SOE better suited to address the case of Chinese SOEs. I showed that the TPP—and then the

[7] Shea (2016).

[8] Blustein (2019), p. 165.

[9] Bhala (2017).

[10] Bhala (2017), pp. 658–659.

[11] Bhala (2017), p. 660.

CPTPP—was the primary example of the new ownership and control framework. Then, the USA took this new definition and applied it as its new legal model, mainly in the 2018 USMCA.

Taking a closer examination of the interplay between the refined definition of SOEs and the primary obligations outlined in the USMCA sheds light on potential implications for economic development policies. Notably, the USMCA introduces Clause 22(7), which imposes restrictions on non-commercial government assistance and actions by SOEs that could result in "adverse effects" on products and services from another Party.

Let me narrow down specifically to Clause 22(7)(a) and (b), which address the production and sale of goods by SOEs that receive any form of non-commercial assistance, such as state-backed, subsidized loans. These clauses signify a deliberate effort to mitigate competition from such SOEs:

> Article 22.7: Adverse Effects 1. For the purposes of Article 22.6.4 and Article 22.6.5 (Non-Commercial Assistance), adverse effects arise if the effect of the non-commercial assistance is:
>
> (a) that the production and sale of a good by a Party's state-owned enterprise that has received the non-commercial assistance displaces or impedes from the Party's market imports of a like good of another Party or sales of a like good produced by an enterprise that is a covered investment in the territory of the Party;
>
> (b) that the production and sale of a good by a Party's state-owned enterprise that has received the non-commercial assistance displaces or impedes from: (i) the market of another Party sales of a like good produced by an enterprise that is a covered investment in the territory of that other Party, or imports of a like good of any other Party, or (ii) the market of a non-Party imports of a like good of another Party.

Clause 22.7(a) within the USMCA specifically targets competition within the home nation of the SOE. It stipulates that if Mexico, for example, provides non-commercial assistance to an SOE, the goods produced by this SOE are prohibited from displacing equivalent goods from the US in the Mexican market. Similarly, it prohibits impeding the entry of similar products into the Mexican market.

Complementing this, Clause 22.7(b) establishes a parallel prohibition against market displacement or entry impediment in the markets of other member states. Hence, goods produced by a subsidized Mexican SOE cannot displace equivalent products from US or Canadian firms in their respective markets. Collectively, these subclauses aim to guarantee market participation.

I would suggest there are potential ramifications for Mexico, for instance. Longstanding economic development policies in Latin American countries, such as import substitution through national SOEs,[12] could face increasing hardships in this context. SOE-produced goods, subsidized by the state to nurture domestic industries and foster a national consumer market, could be rendered prohibited.

It is important to note that the prohibition is not limited to enterprises directly owned by the state but extends to any enterprise over which the government exerts influence, as per the new ownership and control definition of SOEs. This means

[12] Lizarazo-Rodríguez (2021), p. 12.

even the utilization of privately owned enterprises under government direction for industrialization policies would be disallowed. This brief contention hints at a significant potential for new research into how the USMCA paradigm on SOE hinders development policies.

A similar scenario could unfold with the Japanese case. Japan commenced defining SOEs in regional and bilateral trade and investment agreements in 2004, 3 years after China acceded to the WTO.

This was done by applying the ownership and control framework, directly addressing the issue of Chinese SOEs. My analysis reveals that Japan has consistently employed the ownership and control framework in its agreements since then, particularly with nations bordering the Pacific, solidifying a Japanese strategy aimed at creating a regional deterrent against Chinese SOEs.

However, there are also signs of impediment to economic development for underdeveloped nations within Japan's sphere of influence. In hindsight, if South Korea were to have signed an agreement with Japan akin to the 2020 Japan-United Kingdom Comprehensive Economic Partnership Agreement, there could have been conditions in its economic ascent.

I use the example of South Korea to argue that the spread of agreements pushed by Japan offers clues of discouragement for underdeveloped nations in the region from adopting their own domestic policies, an approach resembling South Korea's case of success.

South Korea's industrial success story has been dominated by chaebol enterprises. These conglomerates are characterized by the concentration of ownership and management within the chaebol's founding entrepreneur and their family, operating as family business groups with centralized decision-making processes regarding resource allocation and long-term planning.[13]

However, chaebols have long been accused of benefiting from state favoritism and have been cited as examples of state intervention in the nomination of enterprise officials.[14] These allegations mirror those faced by Chinese SOEs today. In fact, the corporate governance of Chinese SOEs has been influenced by South Korean chaebols as a model of economic development.[15]

Under the 2020 Japan-United Kingdom Comprehensive Economic Partnership Agreement, although privately owned, chaebols could face regulatory treatment similar to SOEs if there is evidence of government influence in their commercial activities. This would subject chaebols to a set of stringent rules they did not encounter during their path to economic success.

For instance, chaebols may be obligated to disclose information about government officials serving in the enterprise and the legal exemptions they benefit from, as outlined in Article 13.7(d) and (e) of the 2020 Japan-United Kingdom Comprehensive Economic Partnership Agreement:

---

[13] Milhaupt (1998), pp. 1162–1163.

[14] Pargendler (2021), pp. 1780–1781.

[15] Gordon and Milhaupt (2019), p. 213.

> Article 13.7 Information Exchange.
>
> 4. The requested Party shall provide the following information, provided that the request includes an explanation of how the activities of the entity may be affecting the interests of the requesting Party under this Chapter and indicates which of the following information shall be provided: (...)
>
> (d) a description of the government departments or public bodies which regulate the entity, a description of the reporting requirements imposed on it by those departments or public bodies, and the rights and practices, where possible, of those departments or public bodies with respect to the appointment, dismissal or remuneration of senior executives and members of its board of directors or any other equivalent management body; (...)
>
> (f) any exemptions, immunities and related measures from which the entity benefits under the laws and regulations of the requested Party.

This increased transparency could expose their connections to government policies and make them susceptible to restrictive measures by trade partners. It could signify the revelation of compelling evidence regarding potential trade-distorting measures by chaebols under the CPTPP, as longstanding accusations have pointed out.

Additionally, it could imply that for countries in the region contemplating the adoption of South Korean strategies for their development, these provisions might significantly diminish the effectiveness of business groups as instruments of industrial policy.

Finally, the EU case follows a similar pattern of clues. It started to introduce a legal definition of SOE in its bilateral and regional trade and investment agreements in 2011—the year in which China consolidated itself as a major source of FDI. It also employed thinner versions of the framework of ownership and control from the beginning, but gradually made the clauses more robust.

The EU presents more evidence that the framework has been thought to regulate Chinese SOEs, because it has agreed in principle on an investment agreement with China. It shows that the framework is, in fact, the chosen one when it comes to defining Chinese SOEs. Still, the EU has also showcased a strong pattern of diffusion of such a framework in agreements that range from East Asia to North America, going through Eastern Europe and the UK.

Together, the cases of the USA, Japan, and the EU call attention to the need to explore the diverse impacts of a unified legal framework on different states, particularly on economies actively engaged in state capital export beyond conventional ownership ties. I believe that the literature has failed to account for the overarching influence of the ownership and control framework upon a diversity of strategies employed by states in utilizing state-owned investment channels.

I contribute to qualify, for example, Babic's delineation of two ideal types of state capital transnationalization strategies, namely, financial and controlling.[16] Babic's assertion that state capital encompasses "all the corporate ownership claims a state possesses"[17] falls short in capturing the intentional breadth of the ownership and control framework.

---

[16] Babic (2023), p. 44.

[17] Babic (2023), p. 42.

China would epitomize what he calls a controlling strategy, in which investment tends to control firms through majority-owned or fully owned.[18] In Babic's view, these are the kind of investments that raise more sensitive political backlash.[19] Portfolio investments by states represent a non-controlling strategy centered on financial returns, circumventing geopolitical tensions.[20]

By employing the control and ownership framework, I demonstrate that, even in the absence of ownership, the government can exert regulatory influence on SOEs. I challenge Babic's exclusive association of control with majority or total ownership. Future research should be encouraged to detail whether there is an effective difference in the legal treatment afforded to SOEs from countries with predominantly financial and controlling strategies.

The evidence presented also underscores that similar legal clauses based on the ownership and control framework are employed across diverse agreements, such as the 2018 USCMA, the 2020 Japan-United Kingdom Comprehensive Economic Partnership Agreement, and the 2017 EU-Armenia Comprehensive and Enhanced Partnership Agreement. I was able to prove that China has sparked an effective convergence between the USA, Japan, and the EU in the construction of a new global pattern of legal definition of SOEs.

References

Babic M (2023) The rise of state capital: transforming markets and international politics. Agenda Publishing Limited, Newcastle

Babic M, Garcia-Bernardo J, Heemskerk EM (2020) The rise of transnational state capital: state-led foreign investment in the 21st century. Rev Int Polit Econ 27(3):433–475

Bhala R (2017) TPP, American National Security and Chinese SOEs. World Trade Rev 16(4):655–671

Blustein P (2019) Schism: China, America and the fracturing of the global trading system. Centre for International Governance Innovation, Waterloo

Gordon JN, Milhaupt CJ (2019) China as a 'National Strategic Buyer': towards a multilateral regime for cross-border M&A. Columb Bus Law Rev 1:192–251

Lizarazo-Rodríguez L (2021) Approaches to law and development. In: de Feyter K, Türkelli GE, de Moerloose S (eds) Encyclopedia of law and development. Elgar Publishing, London, pp 11–15

Milhaupt CJ (1998) Property rights in firms. Va Law Rev 84(6):1145–1194

Pargendler M (2021) The rise of international corporate law. Wash Univ Law Rev 98(6)

Rolland SE, Trubek DM (2019) Emerging Powers in the International Economic Order Cooperation Competition and Transformation Emerging Economies Developmental Strategies and Trade Standards: the Search for Alternative Space Cambridge University Press 136–186.

Shea DC (2016) Testimony of the Honorable Dennis C. Shea Chairman, U.S.-China Economic and Security Review Commission before the U.S. Senate Committee on Banking, Housing, and Urban Affairs Hearing on "Evaluating the Financial Risks of China"

[18] Babic (2023), pp. 44–45.

[19] Babic (2023), p. 36.

[20] Babic et al. (2020), pp. 9–10.

Chapter 5
Concluding Remarks

Abstract China's rise as a global economic power has transformed the legal treatment of state-owned enterprises (SOEs) in trade and investment agreements. This book demonstrates how the United States, the European Union, and Japan shifted from defining SOEs under a governmental authority framework to a stricter ownership and control model. This shift is presented as a strategic recalibration of international economic governance, motivated by concerns over Chinese SOEs' global expansion, market distortions, and national security risks. The analysis highlights that traditional criteria proved inadequate for Chinese firms, which often operate under indirect state influence. As a result, major economies institutionalized new legal rules aimed at constraining China's state-capitalist model. This book makes a key contribution by mapping SOE definitions into three legal approaches — governmental authority, ownership and control, and functional — providing the first systematic foundation for future scholarship. It shows that the ownership and control framework gained dominance not because of inherent superiority but because of its effectiveness in targeting Chinese SOEs, particularly after China's WTO accession. This book also indicates that this framework might disproportionately affect the Global South by limiting long-standing industrialization tools. It also exposes a paradox: while constraining foreign SOEs, advanced economies simultaneously expand state intervention domestically. This reveals SOE regulation as deeply geopolitical, shaping sovereignty, economic governance, and multilateralism. Finally, this book opens new avenues of research on state capitalism, inequality, and the domestic application of these rules.

I have systematically demonstrated how China's ascent as a global economic power has fundamentally reshaped the legal and regulatory treatment of SOEs in international trade and investment agreements.

The book reveals a decisive shift in how major economies—particularly the United States, the European Union, and Japan—have redefined the legal criteria for identifying and regulating SOEs, moving from a traditional governmental authority framework toward a stringent ownership and control model. This transformation represents not merely a technical adjustment but a strategic recalibration of

T. M. Aquino, *SOEs and Global Economic Friction*, SpringerBriefs in Law,
https://doi.org/10.1007/978-3-032-00781-0_5

international economic governance, driven by the perceived need to counterbalance China's state-capitalist system.

At the core of my argument lies the assertion that China's growing influence has served as the primary catalyst for this regulatory shift. Before China's economic rise, SOEs were not uniformly subject to specialized trade disciplines, and definitions varied across agreements. However, as Chinese SOEs expanded globally, developed economies grew increasingly concerned about market distortions, unfair competition, and national security risks.

I illustrate that these concerns were institutionalized into legal frameworks specifically designed to constrain Chinese SOEs' operational flexibility. The transition from the governmental authority framework, which tied SOE status to public functions, to the ownership and control model, which focuses on state shareholding or de facto influence, reflects a deliberate effort to expand regulatory jurisdiction over newer forms of state-backed enterprises. This shift was strategically engineered in response to the practical difficulties of applying traditional criteria to Chinese firms, which often operate under indirect state guidance rather than explicit governmental mandates.

I have made a critical contribution to the field of international economic law and political economy by providing the first comprehensive mapping of SOE definition frameworks. I have organized the previously fragmented literature into three distinct legal approaches—governmental authority, ownership and control, and functional—creating a structured foundation for future scholarship.

Crucially, I demonstrate that the ownership and control framework has emerged as the dominant paradigm not due to inherent superiority but because of its utility in targeting Chinese SOEs. The ownership and control framework proliferated post-2004, coinciding with China's WTO accession and subsequent economic expansion. My data shows that the U.S., EU, and Japan did not merely adopt similar criteria independently but actively converged toward a standardized model, epitomized by the TPP/USMCA and replicated in subsequent agreements.

This convergence challenges the notion that SOE regulation is a neutral, technocratic exercise, instead revealing its deeply geopolitical nature. A critical and underexplored implication of this regulatory shift is its disproportionate impact on developing nations.

By enshrining the ownership and control framework, I showcase possible indications that major economies could restrict policy tools long used by the Global South for industrialization. These indications come as suggestions for future research and increase the relevance of the conclusions presented here, as a new pathway of investigations may arise from it.

My findings expose a striking paradox: even as the U.S., EU, and Japan impose rigid constraints on foreign SOEs, they are simultaneously increasing state intervention in their own economies.[1] This contradiction underscores that the ownership and

[1] Juhász et al. (2023).

control framework is not merely about ensuring competitive neutrality but about reshaping global economic governance under market-based regulatory preferences while retaining domestic policy flexibility.

The convergence of the U.S., the European Union, and Japan represents not an accident of legal evolution but a deliberate geoeconomic strategy—one that redefines the rules of trade to manage the challenges posed by China's state-led model while possibly constraining developmental policies in the Global South. The implications extend far beyond SOEs, touching upon core debates about sovereignty, economic governance, and the future of multilateralism.

As the international order grapples with competing visions of capitalism, the book provides a crucial foundation for understanding how law is weaponized in great-power competition—and who bears the costs of this regulatory transformation.

Looking forward, I aim to open several avenues for further inquiry, including examinations of how the ownership and control framework differentially affects various models of state capitalism, whether this regulatory convergence exacerbates global economic inequalities, and how advanced economies navigate these rules in their own domestic contexts.

Reference

Juhász R, Lane NJ, Rodrik D (2023) The new economics of industrial policy. NBER Working Paper Series, No. August

Made in the USA
Monee, IL
18 October 2026

66037391R00050